THE TRANSFORMED ABBOT

Abbot Miao-Chi in ceremonial dress

THE
TRANSFORMED
ABBOT

by

KARL REICHELT

Translated by
G. M. REICHELT
and
A. P. ROSE

LUTTERWORTH PRESS

LONDON

First published 1954

This book is a shortened translated version of the original, which appeared as Volume II of "Fromhetstyper og Helligdommer i Ost-Asia", Dreyers Forlag, Oslo.

Printed in Great Britain by
The Camelot Press Ltd., London and Southampton

PREFACE

THE LARGEST AND most comprehensive of China's religions, Buddhism, has long been normative in the Far East because of the richness of its thought revealed in wide expressions of devotional life and organization. It may be of interest to the West to see a living picture-gallery of Buddhist monks and laymen, but as the picture unfolds it will be seen to be organically related to one central figure; a man in many respects unique and richly endowed, the Buddhist monk Miao-Chi,[1] whose studies, travels and life-work took place in Formosa (Taiwan), Japan and China.

Of the many thousand monks with whom the author made contact during his forty-three years in China, Miao-Chi was one of the most outstanding in religious disposition, earnestness and spiritual gifts. Being so prominent, Miao-Chi came into contact with those outstanding persons and movements that moulded the Buddhist world in East Asia from the turn of the present century. It is with deep sorrow that the main features of his life are described, for this promising friend, who progressed so far not only in general religious insight but in Christian faith and knowledge, passed away just when, humanly speaking, he was most needed.

The most important source for describing Miao-Chi's life has been the careful notes I made as he described his career openly and without reserve during our time together on the Island of Formosa. Some details are from my memory. To these have been added valuable materials which his fellow-monks gave me in Formosa and Shanghai. Diaries and letters provided useful data, as did copies of the periodical *Ya-Kuang* ("Asia's Light") which Miao-Chi initiated and edited in Formosa. Finally must be mentioned talks with Dr. R. B. McClure and other missionaries who knew and helped my friend.

For this English edition warm thanks are due to my friend, the Rev. H. F. Wickings, of the London Missionary Society, who has

---

[1] Pronounced "Mee-ów-chee" (with accent on second syllable.)

shortened the material and re-arranged it in chronological order. He has not only improved the English throughout the book but, from his personal knowledge, has checked and brought up to date certain descriptions of events and places. This has proved invaluable.

KARL LUDVIG REICHELT.

TAO FENG SHAN,
SHATIN, HONG KONG.
January 1952.

Shortly after Dr. Reichelt wrote his preface he passed away in the Brotherhood which he had established at Tao Feng Shan. His passing was a grievous loss to religion and scholarship in the Far East. No other Westerner in living memory possessed such insight into Buddhism and its practices, nor exercised so great a Christian influence upon Buddhist monks and leaders, for his understanding and sympathy bridged the gulf between the two religions.

Despite the Communist Revolution of 1948-49 Buddhism still lives in China. Pilgrimages are restricted and frowned upon, some of the temples have been turned into schools by the People's Government, and numbers of monks have been ejected as "unproductive"—so that they now have to earn their living on the streets of Chinese cities as boot-blacks and hairdressers, but the strength of modern Buddhism, as Dr. Reichelt emphasizes, lies in its laymen's movement. If the new regime fails to meet the religious needs of the people Buddhism may well fulfil some of those needs and hold its own. As China's history shows, Buddhism is usually able to adapt itself to the new day.

H. F. W.

CONTENTS

NOVICE IN FORMOSA

1

At Home in Ta Hu

IN ONE OF Formosa's remote mountain valleys lies the village of Ta Hu ("Great Lake"), so called from its proximity to the large sheet of water occupying the floor of the valley. After two hours' rail travel southwards from Taipeh, the capital of the island, a change is made at Piao Miao to a branch line that runs southeast. This line is of narrow gauge on which runs a hand-propelled trolley where two or three passengers and a conductor can stand or squat. Travel on this primitive, switchback line tends to be hair-raising, but the loveliness of the scenery more than compensates for possible shocks to the nerves. Ta Hu village stands in a singularly beautiful position. Towards the east are mountains and virgin forest. To the south and west the valley opens towards the lake and there are many paddy fields. In summer, when there are often cloudbursts and typhoons, the mountain streams bring down such torrents of water that the lake rises and floods some of the fields and pastures. Then the local people imagine that Lung Wang ("the Dragon King") is angry, and they go in procession with offerings in order to appease his wrath. It is significant that the earliest and finest temple near by is dedicated to Lung Wang. A belt of light green bamboo divides jungle from village. From a distance this bamboo grove adds attraction to the landscape by bringing into relief the deep blue of the lake and the lighter tinge of the mountains. Rice is reaped twice a year and in winter tall sugar canes sway in the wind.

Chinese colonists, chiefly from Fukien and Kuangtung, settled down several hundred years ago on the level coastal lands of Formosa and their successors had perforce to struggle inland among the mountain valleys. On the lofty mountain plateau itself live primitive Formosan tribes whose main interest is hunting. Until recent years they have also hunted human beings in order to obtain as many skulls as possible because these are supposed to bring strength and power. It must have been a risky adventure for Chinese colonists to settle in the mountain valleys, and careful watch was always necessary.

Many immigrants from South China during the later period were Hakkas (Chinese, *k'eh-chia*, meaning "stranger people"), a pushful type that originally came from North China many centuries ago. Amongst them was a family with the surname of Lo. This family settled at Ta Hu, and because they were industrious it was not long before they were able to build a family home surrounded by gardens, and with ricefields, in well-constructed terraces, reaching down to the lake. One of this family towards the end of last century was called Lo Wan-Ssu, and he was an able and outstanding scholar. He married a thrifty and gifted Hakka woman who eventually became the mother of three sons, Chi-Ying ("manful hero") Fu-Ying ("prospering hero") and Tao-Ying ("hero of truth"). The father was often absent on government duties and the mother had to carry the chief responsibility in the home. She was a woman of high ideals and gave her children a good home and the best possible education. She burnt incense for ancestors and heavenly spirits on the home altar and placed an extra altar by the side of the ancestral tablets. This was for Kuan-Yin, the Goddess of Mercy, and there every night she recited from the Heart Sutra and the Book of the Merciful Vows of Amitabha.

The youngest son, Tao-Ying, was born in 1895. He was the one who showed greatest interest in his mother's devotions, and, being a bright lad, he learnt passages by heart. He was, however, inclined to be hot-headed and led his comrades in many pranks. Still, everybody knew that he was a kind fellow, and for that reason children and grown-ups became fond of him, although some remarked that there was "something peculiar about that lad".

This was possibly due to the fact that Tao-Ying began more and more to seek solitude in the forest or in some quiet spot in the mountains. Often he would sit contemplating the landscape while solemnity, sadness, feelings of unworthiness and awe, as well as joy and pain, came over him.

At school all three brothers were successful. Fu-Ying seemed gifted for practical work, so it was decided that he should stay at home and look after the farm. Chi-Ying, the eldest, and Tao-Ying, the youngest, appeared to be destined for study.

A great event in the Ta Hu district was the building of a large Buddhist monastery on one of the mountains close by. Several wealthy Chinese had met together under the leadership of two energetic monks. They had stressed the importance of such an enterprise because it would check the wild mountaineers who had the utmost respect for holy places. Within two years the new building, Fa Yün Ssu ("Law's Cloud Monastery", from the Buddhist idea of doctrine or law; Sanscrit, *dharma*), with its spacious halls, stood ready for occupation. Lo Wan-Ssu came home for the solemn inauguration lasting several days. It became an event not to be forgotten by Tao-Ying. An urge to enter upon monastic life seemed to grow in his consciousness but he knew that unless something important happened he would never be able to take this decisive step.

In school there were radical changes. The Japanese, who had taken over Formosa in 1895, had many problems of administration and amongst the first issues they took up was the school system. During the first four years of Tao-Ying's education everything was conducted in the old style. An old teacher recited the classics in a monotonous chant. Afterwards each of his pupils stood with his back to the teacher and recited in the same chanting manner what the teacher had said. Character writing with a brush occupied the rest of the time. Gradually such boys became scholars with a knowledge of the rules of moral conduct based upon a philosophy of life ages old when the world at large, nature study and the history of mankind remained a closed book. This suddenly changed. New teachers, educated at the Normal College, appeared at the ancestral home of the Lo clan. Its main hall was divided into smaller classrooms and the whole institution turned into a modern middle school. A new curriculum, comprising geography, history, natural science, advanced arithmetic, dietetics and singing, appeared; and in addition to Chinese the study of Japanese became a compulsory subject. Pictures and maps, as well as drawings illustrating the flora and fauna of Asia, decorated the walls. There were periods for sport and gymnastics. Tao-Ying was enraptured. He drank in the new knowledge.

Life in school absorbed most of his time and thought, and it was only during holidays that he could go for solitary walks. Each vacation seemed to mean a new home-coming spiritually. Solitary hours of meditation in the mountains, while temple bells from the new monastery resounded through the valley, helped to relieve the tension and strain of study. His eldest brother, Chi-Ying, had been studying for some time in the capital, while Fu-Ying had become a farmer who in spare time studied new methods of agriculture. Tao-Ying himself was preparing for middle school examinations when a serious event shook him.

Their beloved mother fell seriously ill. Tao-Ying, always sensitive of mind, became indefatigable in attendance at the sick-bed, and when he had finished his schooling and was preparing to enter college he firmly declared, "Not so long as mother is ill!" The illness became protracted, and everybody could see that her powers of resistance were weakening. Lo Wan-Ssu returned home and secured a post as teacher in Chinese at the school so as to be near his wife. Friends and neighbours came often to see the patient.

One day the Abbot from the new monastery came to inquire for Mother Lo, and Tao-Ying noticed that he had a long private talk with his parents. The Abbot's contention was that doctors and medicine could not save the mother; only one remedy remained. At this point he gave the parents a searching look. Heaven had bestowed upon them three excellent sons; the eldest was attending college in the capital, the next was looking after the farm and thus fully occupied, but the youngest, a gifted youth, should possibly be the one to represent the clan as a monk. By dedicating himself to such a life he might be able to save his mother. The patient glanced at her husband in a meaningful way, indicating that her inmost thoughts had been expressed. Father Lo, realizing the situation, merely said that they would have to think it over.

During the next three days Lo Wan-Ssu ate hardly anything but went for long walks in the mountains or confined himself to his room. On the fourth day he solemnly entered the sickroom looking very grave. At the same time his face possessed a certain radiance; he had fought his battle and obtained peace. In a low voice he said to his wife, "Surely the best thing will be to follow the Abbot's advice." Tao-Ying was then called in and the decision announced by the father. He felt convinced, he said, that

Tao-Ying, who had always been an example of *hsiao* ("filial piety"), would comply with the wish of his parents. He had noticed Tao-Ying's propensity towards solitude and the calm of a temple atmosphere, and was therefore confident that the decision was in full accord with the will of Heaven. For Tao-Ying all this came as a complete surprise but he felt it to be in harmony with his longings and aspirations. Consequently he made up his mind there and then, and instantly felt calm and happy, a feeling which spread to the others. The patient too experienced a brief improvement in vitality, and even when her illness took a firmer grip she felt as if all her sorrows and anxieties had been removed.

2

The Mark of Buddha

AFTER A COUPLE of weeks the sixteen-year-old Tao-Ying
had settled as a novice in Fa Yün Ssu. The lay robe had been put
aside, his head shaved and Tao-Ying ("hero of truth") had become
Miao-Chi ("mysterious joy"). No less a person than the Abbot
himself became his master. This at once placed Miao-Chi in a
position which in time might open up access to high rank.
Seldom has a young man in East Asia entered a monastery on a
more secure footing. He was also fortunate in entering such a
monastery. At that time there was gathered at Fa Yün Ssu a rare
group of intelligent young monks, and the Abbot had built up
an excellent staff of teachers. Discipline was good and the spirit
and tone stood considerably above the ordinary monastic level.

Three months of residence made Miao-Chi feel at home in the
monastery. He had got into the routine and felt well both
physically and spiritually. The only shadow was his mother's
illness, which had now taken on a more threatening character.
Six months after he entered the monastery she died peacefully.

At the funeral, in addition to the most important members of
the Lo clan, the whole complement of monks attended. The proceedings were conducted with immense solemnity. Lo Wan-Ssu
and his three sons, dressed in white mourning and bowed down
with sorrow, followed next to the coffin and were supported by
their male relatives, while a group of women relatives played the
part of weeping maidens. A band of flute-players and gong-
beaters followed, and at intervals salvoes of crackers were discharged. After the funeral all gathered in an open place where
were set out horses, vehicles and retinues of servants carrying
hand-baggage, all ingeniously constructed of paper stretched over
frames of thin bamboo. After an act of devotion these were all set

on fire, and thus the deceased would have all she required for her travels through the land of shadows. In short, the whole complicated ceremonial in connection with Chinese funeral customs was followed, a sad mingling of superstition, theatrical artifice and sincerely-felt sorrow. This was not all; for three days special masses for the dead were sung in the main hall of the monastery by a large body of monks. This was reckoned the most important part of the funeral ceremony, because, according to popular Buddhist conception, it was these masses which would help the deceased to burst open the gates of death; they would propitiate Yen-Lo, the severe Judge of the Kingdom of Death, and give the soul "wings to soar above and beyond the iron grip of the *Karma* wheel".[1] These long and monotonous masses often sink into mere routine, but for Miao-Chi the whole affair meant much more. With a sincerity that came to influence him for life he applied himself to these devotions with fastings and vigils so that both the Abbot and other leaders became anxious for his health.

The entire first year in the monastery became of importance to Miao-Chi. He willingly underwent severe self-discipline and as never before he fought his quick temper. There came a new earnestness and dignity into his nature, and his comrades noted with increasing wonder how he began to bridle his tongue and how even in the midst of business he took time for meditation in the courtyard of the monastery.

After one year he was ordained and received "the mark of Buddha" on his head.[2] This meant that he could now study the Buddhist scriptures, and under skilled guidance he made considerable progress in this direction. Later came practical work, for it was important to learn the intricate administration of a modern monastery, such as book-keeping, the purchase of supplies, storing, secretarial work, the duties of host, and so on. He rather dreaded the last of these and breathed more freely when he was relieved of it. In that short time he had come to realize the many dangers and temptations to which this position is open.

Visitors come from town and country districts in order to request masses for their dead. A special group of monks, who do not enter the school department, conduct the masses, but the

[1] See detailed descriptions of these names in K. L. Reichelt's *Truth and Tradition in Chinese Buddhism*, pp. 67-111.

[2] On ordination see *op. cit.*, pp. 228-39.

duties of hospitality are performed by one of the more prominent and literary of the monks. Some visitors are sincere in their devotions, both on their own behalf and on behalf of their relatives, whereas others make use of their stay in the temple chiefly as a holiday or an opportunity for amusement. The diet is, of course, necessarily limited to vegetarian dishes but in compensation wealthier families often bring wine and opium. Many families cannot think of spending days in a monastery without shortening the time by gambling. So there often develops not only wine-bibbing but a lot of gambling and night orgies, and with this night life other evils follow. Consequently, the host, deputy host, and monastery servants are often placed in great difficulty. They have to see that there is quiet and order but they do not care to offend rich and distinguished visitors lest that should adversely affect the generous giving which is expected from such folk. Miao-Chi felt an abyss open before him several times. What helped him during the strain was the image of his devoted mother; he felt that he thus received power to avoid the temptation.

Fa Yün Ssu followed the usual practice with regard to devotions. At three o'clock in the morning drums and bells sounded to call the monks to assembly in the main hall. They would proceed with almost soundless step through the long corridors for morning mass lasting an hour and a half. Then came breakfast in the refectory about five o'clock. The forenoon was spent in various kinds of practical work. Midday meal was taken at eleven o'clock. After this a monk could rest or attend to private affairs until common meditation began about three o'clock. Those belonging to the school department were exempt from this as they continued with their studies. Evening meal followed the final mass about six o'clock. During the night individual monks took prayer-watches in turn, sitting in the bell-tower or in the sanctuary. They recited in low tones the Ti-Ts'ang Scripture, the special one that is read to obtain help and release for lost spirits in the torture chamber of the Kingdom of Death (*yu-ming-ku*). At certain intervals a particular iron bell would be struck for the benefit of those unhappy spirits, and a deep boom would reverberate into the night for over a minute. One needs to be present in such a monastery to appreciate the atmosphere, charged with solemnity, which the sounding of these bells carries with it.

Miao-Chi soon became one of the leaders among the younger

monks, and in addition to his work in the school was given a good many literary tasks in the Abbot's study. He was exempt from the prayer-watch and some of the other routine. This gave him opportunity for pressing on with private studies and provided him with leisure for walking in the mountains. Solitude became more and more precious to him as the riddles of life pressed upon him. Constant reading, studies in school and contact with many different monks who came on visits from China and Japan, the political tension in connection with the First World War, all helped to keep his sensitive heart and acute mind active. When he had learned all that could be learned in the Formosan monastery a longing for the outside world began to surge up within him. His superiors and his family understood this, and it was eventually decided that he should be allowed to go to Japan and China for further study.

PILGRIM IN JAPAN

3

Valley of Cedars

IT WAS IN June 1918 that Miao-Chi stepped ashore at the port of Yokohama, near Tokyo. He was now twenty-three years old. It had been arranged that he should spend a few months in the capital where he would obtain useful impressions of modern Japan. For that reason he did not immediately settle down in a Buddhist monastery but took up quarters in a large hostel for students from Formosa.

After two months Miao-Chi took up residence in one of Tokyo's chief monasteries, the Kwannon Temple in Asakusa Park. The external arrangements were a model of efficiency and elegance and a number of the monks were alert and intelligent. It was impressive to watch the large crowds that surged in and out daily through the sanctuaries. True, quite a number were only tourists, but there were schoolchildren too, led by their teachers, and large numbers of Buddhist societies from country districts carrying banners. They all made a brief reverence in front of the main altar and threw a few coppers into a fenced receptacle for alms. Occasionally silver and paper money would be thrown in. Some people gave themselves more time and sat or knelt in prayer or leaned back in order to meditate. They were mostly women, but some were men. Miao-Chi noticed how quickly the people finished their devotions and how their whole manner betrayed vacancy of mind. It became obvious that the spiritual atmosphere of Tokyo was unfavourable to religious life. It was still more depressing for him to see the attitude of mind displayed by the monks. Intelligent young monks appeared to spend all too much of their time engaged in one or other of the numerous societies and organizations, simply because it was not done to stand aloof; the new Japan demanded it. Older monks had to take some share too because Buddhism must needs accommodate itself to new conditions. Hence "accommodation" became the slogan in educational programmes, in speeches, in ritual and not least in all Buddhist literature issued from the capital.

When Miao-Chi discovered a couple of monks who seemed more sincerely disposed, he spoke frankly about his impressions. Instead of replying these two led him to their private cell, for such things could not be spoken of openly, and there they opened their hearts to him. "What you mention", they said, "is a great sorrow to several of us. The Shintō movement is now all powerful and we are forced to follow as best we may. It is the more to be deplored as we clearly discern that Buddhism and Confucianism have a holy duty to perform in Japan, and that is to defend the ethical laws which lie at the roots of world order. We know too that Buddhism has the special task of stressing the supernatural ideal in order to prevent all strife. The very heart of our religion is understanding, love and mercy. But what can we do in such times? We understand that you have come to Japan to study the inner character of religion. Well, you have come to the wrong place. You should visit our holy Koyasan and that real heart of Buddhism in Japan, Kyoto. There you will meet people who will understand you and share your interests."

Koyasan ("High Mountain in the Wilderness") corresponds very well to its name, as it stands high and isolated, surrounded by thick forest.

The monastic buildings are surrounded by dense groves of cypress, acacias and cedars. Miao-Chi was allowed to stay in a monastery that stands secluded in a side valley. Its temple halls are of unique beauty as several of Japan's most prominent artists have decorated the walls with frescoes. Among them is a gigantic picture, painted about five hundred years ago by the monk artist Sotan, of "Plum Tree in Blossom." It occupies one long wall of the main hall and one of the ends. Anything more alive than this fresco could scarcely be imagined. Groups of people are always sitting on mats before it in contemplation. Hour after hour they sit and take in the peculiar poetry of life which "Plum Tree in Blossom" proclaims.

Not far away stands the main temple of the Shingon School. This temple, together with one other from which the master Kobodaishi is said to have entered Nirvana, shows the high lights of Koyasan's peculiar architecture. For instance, there is an impressive fresco that draws thousands in the pilgrim season. It is a winter landscape, "Willow Tree in Snow", and occupies one of the long walls. Other walls are covered with colossal renderings of scenes from Buddha's life or the activity of the Law of Life (*fa-chieh*) in the hearts of men and in destiny. Most fearful of all is the rendering of the Wheel of Karma. The setting is provided by a loathsome monster. The highest sector of the wheel is dominated by the face of this creature which has sunk its fangs deeply into the body of the world. With its fore claws the monster clutches the top section of the wheel and with its two terrible hind paws the monster holds the lower part. In other words, the monster has complete power over the world and mankind. This is the law of sin in operation, but there is another side because the law of salvation is in operation too. Below is a dark and muddy pool, and a good seed from above has settled in its sediment. Roots are going down while a tender stem makes its way upwards to light, and on the surface of the water spreads out a pure and fragrant lotus lily. Thus a human soul has come to enlightenment and peace.

Miao-Chi realized that the spiritual atmosphere in Koyasan was much better than in the capital. There was more concentration, more inwardness and sincerity spent over the devotions and hours of meditation. It was not long before he found friends among the monks. One of them proved to be no less than the leader of the School of Shingon's seminary, the pious and learned Takahashi. At the outset of their meeting Miao-Chi explained the motives of his visit to Koyasan; he wished to meet monks who had had a personal religious experience, and he would appreciate in particular learning what special methods and viewpoints the School of Mystery adhered to in order to obtain valuable experiences. Takahashi received Miao-Chi with great friendliness; evidently there was something in the young man's nature that immediately inspired confidence. He was careful not to enter into profound problems and explanations immediately; he had his own method. He first took Miao-Chi around those places on the mountain connected with the founder of the Shingon School, Kobodaishi ("Great Teacher Kobo"), a master highly honoured in Japan.

Kobodaishi lived from A.D. 774-835 and visited China where he studied intently the School of Mystery (Chinese, *mi-tsung*), then high in esteem. He made a long stay in Ch'angan (now Sian). It is possible that he came into contact with Nestorian Christians who were then prominent in and around Ch'angan. Kobodaishi was broad-minded, and it is perhaps significant that after his return to Japan he made the Sun Scripture (*ta-rih-ching*) the chief scripture of the Shingon School. At the same time he promoted the cause of Confucianism in Japan because he found that Confucianism had a considerable contribution to make towards the development of a sound communal morality. It amplified the one-sided interpretation of the development of life as taught by Shintōism, and was complementary to Buddhism with its more personal conception of Heaven. Kobodaishi was one of the most remarkable religious figures which Japan has produced, a man who influenced her spiritual life in the most diverse fields. In particular he developed his beloved Koyasan into the most important religious centre of his time. To begin with, Miao-Chi did not understand why the fatherly Takahashi laid such emphasis on showing him all the places connected with Kobodaishi's life. Later it dawned upon him that he wished Miao-Chi's inner self to come under Kobodaishi's spiritual power and thereby share in its blessing.

Takahashi described what Kobodaishi experienced when he obtained enlightenment sitting under one of the mighty cedar trees. This spot has naturally become one of the most notable in Koyasan, and noble families have reserved certain areas as burial grounds for themselves. Here are mausoleums where funerary urns of famous monks are kept, and at the southern end of the grove is the mausoleum for Kobodaishi himself. This place is reckoned specially meritorious for pilgrims to worship in. Over the expanse stand immense numbers of cedar trees. They are of the species known as Cryptomeria Japonica which sometimes reaches a height of one hundred and twenty to one hundred and sixty feet. Even the lightest wind sets their crowns in motion, so that a constant rustling and whispering is heard throughout the valley day and night, like a muted organ playing a solemn requiem for the dead. Miao-Chi never tired of wandering in the valley.

At one monument in particular Miao-Chi had to stop again and again. It was a well-executed cast of the Nestorian Tablet found in 1625 at Sian (formerly Ch'angan), the capital of the Province of Shensi in China. The monument was erected in A.D. 781 and the original is now preserved in the Museum of

Antiquities, Peiling, in Sian. The tablet gives a short description of the expansion of Christianity as far as Ch'angan (then the capital of the whole of China) under the Syrian missionary, Alopen, in A.D. 635. The inscription gives an exposition of the message of Christianity. The whole is written in a choice style, but, in order to express the religious content of Christianity, it was necessary to make use of Buddhist and Taoist expressions. This monument thereby gained a dignified colour and clothing of language which secured for it a high place in the minds of the literati of East Asia.

Prior to this experience Miao-Chi had not realized the significance of Christianity. Occasionally he had seen Christians going to service in Formosa, and had listened once or twice to Christian open-air speakers, but what he had heard seemed to him only vague figures of speech. It became still worse when some Christian leaflets came into his hands, because they were in language so simple and formless, without poetry or dignity.

Here was something quite different; deep religious thoughts concerning the Divine seeking man, of light and life being incarnate in Christ Jesus and of the divine Spirit who gives the highest wisdom and dispels the darkness of despair. And all this told in a style so exalted that each word became as music.

Miao-Chi read and re-read the text, and in astonishment turned to Takahashi saying, "How was it that this ancient Christian monument came to be set up in the middle of Kobodaishi's funeral grove?"

Takahashi replied that the original monument, which had been found some miles outside Ch'angan, had evidently stood near one of the Nestorian sanctuaries and had been dedicated about the time when Kobodaishi was living in Ch'angan district. With the close connection which then existed between Buddhists and Nestorians one might well imagine that the master had attended the ceremony. Further, in Kobodaishi's written works are a number of terms and expressions which are reminiscent of the text of the Nestorian Tablet. Takahashi, as one of Koyasan's foremost literati, had had a good deal to do with the dedication ceremony of the replica and was familiar with the history of the original. He pointed out to Miao-Chi that the School of Mystery had developed just at that time into a new sect known as the great Sun Religion (Chinese, *ta rih chiao*) a name which resembles the designation of the Nestorian Church. This first Christian Church in China was called in Chinese *Ching-chiao*, usually rendered "the luminous religion". The adjective *ching* (luminous) is composed of two characters, one for metropolis or great and the other meaning the sun. The resemblance to "great sun religion" is striking. Hence the sight of this beautiful replica of the Nestorian Tablet became a milestone in Miao-Chi's life and whenever possible he made a daily visit to study the text.

From an orthodox Christian viewpoint there is much to criticize in its rendering of the content of the Faith. The central points concerning the Atonement perfected on Calvary by Jesus Christ, the Resurrection and the giving of the Spirit at Pentecost are only vaguely indicated. Other important points are either omitted or so much toned down that the Gospel does not stand out in full clearness and power. Moreover there are indications of points of view which are strange to the Christian world of ideas. Christians feel all these to be shortcomings. Nevertheless those with more sense of the history of religion feel profoundly grateful that at such an early time in China's church history there could be produced a monument which gave, relatively, so much Christian truth.

4

Under Suzuki's Guidance

FROM KOYASAN MIAO-CHI went to Kyoto and to the home
of Professor Suzuki, who taught Zen Buddhism and History of
Religion in the famous Otani College, in a peaceful quarter near
the botanical gardens. The Professor sat in a corner of his garden
deep in meditation. His serious face was calm and mild but at the
same time the lines of his mouth showed signs of energy and
firmness. It was, however, when the eyes of the Professor first
rested on him that Miao-Chi gained the full impression of peculiar
charm, for those eyes lit up his face at the same time as they
expressed intelligence and warmness of heart. Miao-Chi felt that
he could speak frankly about everything and therefore hid
nothing. He spoke of his religious doubts and difficulties and of
his experiences at Tokyo and Koyasan. He dwelt at length upon
the powerful impression which the Nestorian tablet had made
upon him. When he spoke of this Suzuki's face brightened and
he exclaimed, "How interesting that you have come into contact
with Christianity in this way! Yes, it has much to give us, but
remember that only he who has come to a right understanding of
Zen Buddhism can receive a full blessing from Christianity as
well as from other great religions!"

Miao-Chi had often wished that he could devote himself with
the inwardness of faith to the "All-Father Buddha" (Amitabha)
whom the Buddhism of the Pure Land School proclaims, for he
had seen how pious Buddhists had found in that way a wonderful
source of joy and peace both in the struggle of life and before the
gates of death. Yet there had always been something to hold him
back. There was no historical basis for the Amitabha idea; it was,
he felt, no more than a myth. Possibly Zen, the way of the
Meditation School (Chinese, *Ch'an*), was safer, a mystical experience which comes by penetration into one's own being through

personal effort and there finds a reflection of the basic pattern of life. He now heard from his new master that there exists a higher synthesis of these two apparently contradictory ways of salvation. Something of this he had recently felt when he stood face to face with the Nestorian Tablet on Koyasan.

To everyone who came into close contact with Suzuki it was obvious that Christ played a great part in his life and thoughts, either because he was goaded into opposition by a number of sayings in the New Testament, or that in Christ he had found an absolute criterion. It is significant of his attitude to Christ that he always emphasized the importance for students at the college to grasp every opportunity of studying the figure of Christ Jesus. When he learnt that the present writer was willing to speak on religion in the light of Buddhism and Christianity he immediately undertook to arrange a gathering of professors and students from the various colleges and monasteries in Kyoto. The lecture was held in the festival hall at Otani College and hundreds of students and professors attended. Suzuki took the chair and translated the lecture into Japanese. It became an uplifting occasion, not least because of Suzuki's concluding speech in which he stressed what Jesus means to the world.

5

With the Brotherhood of Nishida

THROUGH PROFESSOR SUZUKI Miao-Chi heard about the "Francis of Japan", Tenko Nishida, who, like another Christian pioneer, Kagawa, opened up new ways of saving and helping the neglected and needy.

Originally a business man, Nishida did not have opportunities to pursue far-reaching studies. He merely received an ordinary education like any other Japanese belonging to the middle class; but, possessing a keen religious disposition, he appears to have absorbed much of the teachings of Shintōism, Confucianism and Buddhism.

Evidently the latter religion meant a great deal to him. It was, however, Christianity which called forth his peculiar religious zeal. Now and then he had come into contact with Christians, but never in such a way as to receive a thorough and systematic instruction in Christianity. He managed to provide himself with a copy of the New Testament, and it is clear from his life and from the booklet he wrote that Nishida imbibed deep draughts from this source. He was greatly impressed by a book on Francis of Assisi. This book became to him, as well as to Kagawa, a decisive influence.

When he became mature he experienced a serious religious crisis and this resulted in a clear "cosmic awakening". It must have taken place about the year 1902 because in the following year he founded the society of *It-to-en* ("Society of Witness to Unity"). The name pointed to something profound in Nishida's programme, and that was the gathering of all who were truly religious into a united brotherhood for the salvation and uplift of the needy. It also aimed at overcoming selfishness, lust and self-indulgence in others by going right into the camp of the enemy with the reconciling word and a self-sacrificial mind, which make a man ready and patient to take upon himself the sins and waywardness of others.

Nishida discovered, during his contacts with Buddhists and Christians, that there really were some people who had experienced divine power but for the most part they had not found one another. Hence they could not march forward with a united front. True, there were plenty of large and beautiful temples and churches, plenty of rituals and external forms such as parades and pilgrimages, but all too little determined and self-sacrificial work where the need was greatest. His watchwords therefore became simplicity, austerity, willing self-sacrifice and humility. Love must characterize the lives of the brothers and sisters. Their dwellings, their meals, their clothing and houses of worship must be marked by simplicity. When a team of workers gathers for common meals and devotion everything must be conducted, as far as possible, in silence. Their place of meeting must be a combined meditation and dining hall. Ordinarily there is no altar in this hall, simply a tablet with the inscription "Not two", meaning there is one God behind everything.

In the early morning they gather for devotions and a frugal breakfast; afterwards they go out to serve the sick, the poor and the destitute. At sunset those who are able return to their common home. After the evening meal and devotions they exchange experiences and make plans for the following day while some are sent out for special night work in the slums. The members of this peculiar brotherhood do not wear any special dress but go around in simple kimonos and generally have straw sandals on their feet.

Nishida wrote of the Brotherhood:

> Inwardly our Society lives by penitence; outwardly it lives by service which asks for no return. Of course this is not all. If we compare our society with the life of a family it is reminiscent not so much of a stern father as of the mother. In the life of mankind there is so little of this tender-hearted side because men in their selfishness continually wage wars of various sorts and continually sink deeper into confusion and darkness.
>
> People have found that our Society possesses the power to solve life's most complicated difficulties. I found the way to my present position not through any special education, nor from traditional beliefs, nor did I follow any special teaching; the truth came when my own life was illuminated by heavenly light. It came to me like a flash of lightning when, as an uneducated

business man, I went through a great crisis and was driven to forsake riches, worldly hopes and even my own home.

Nishida's brotherhood home in Kyoto made a tremendous impression upon Miao-Chi. He did not rest content but again and again went up at dusk to the spot where this unusual team of men and women gathered in their working clothes for quiet devotion and deliberation. Miao-Chi was fortunate enough one day to meet the leader himself as Tenko Nishida arrived in Kyoto on a tour of inspection. This meeting Miao-Chi reckoned later to be one of his life's greatest experiences. He wrote to his eldest brother:

> For a long time I have been visiting at nightfall the Society for Witness to Unity and I must say that a more noble and self-sacrificial people I have never met. These brothers have taken up in earnest the thoughts of Christ for saving mankind. Strange how again and again of late I have come into contact with Christ, the world's greatest *bodhisattva*; first on Koyasan, then with my master Suzuki and through the books he lent me about Francis of Assisi, but now in a special way through the founder of the Witness Society, Tenko Nishida. This man came here himself to inspect the work. It struck me the moment I saw him; here one stands face to face with a prophet, a rare and holy man! I was so overcome that I threw myself at his feet but he immediately came forward and raised me up, saying, "Do not bow down to me but adore the Blessed One who gave his life for us on the Cross in order that we should all become one."
>
> Afterwards we sat down and talked together, and I shall never forget the visions he unfolded to me. I mention this to you because I feel that his utterances will be like a shining star guiding me henceforward.

6

At "The Heart's Mysterious Unfolding"

DEPRESSED BY HIS visits to some of the Kyoto monasteries, Miao-Chi entered a monastery of the Zen Buddhist school noted for discipline and order, situated outside the boundaries of the town. Miao-Hsin-ji was the name of the place ("Monastery of the Heart's Mysterious Unfolding"). The locality was quiet and attractive and the number of monks limited to thirty. Its leader in 1920 was a devout and able man. All manual work was carried out by the monks themselves. Here the time was minutely apportioned between manual work, devotion, study and meditation. Diet was strictly vegetarian, but simple, wholesome and nourishing; the cells and halls were like all the other rooms, airy and clean, and great emphasis was placed upon the education of the monks and an understanding of hygiene. The monastery may therefore be said to have been a model place for any who wished to concentrate the mind and penetrate to enlightenment (*satori*).

It was not easy at first for Miao-Chi to follow the day's programme of the monastery, having now enjoyed freedom for a considerable length of time, but it was not long before he came into line with the other monks. After two months he felt it to be a physical and spiritual attraction to go to the hall of meditation when the bell summoned and to sit down cross-legged for several hours. He could not always follow slavishly the details given by the instructor in regard to the sequence of thought which should be followed. His spiritual horizon was too wide for that, but it always brought spiritual reward to be alone in silence with his thoughts and face to face with the innermost meaning and relationships of life.

At the outset he had felt something of the usual insecurity in having to launch out upon the "limitless ocean of meditation", and the talk of giving up and forgetting self sounded to his ears dangerous and unnatural until he experienced what lay behind it.

The memorable day was May 25, 1920, some weeks before he was due to end his stay in Japan and proceed to China. It was a lovely day and the doors and windows of the meditation hall stood wide open so that the refreshing air of early summer could sweep in. The fragrance of lilies drifted in from the garden and the twittering of birds could be heard in the distance.

At the midday break Miao-Chi had read a Japanese pamphlet, *Life in the Light of Eternity*. The author's name was not given but Miao-Chi felt he must be a man well acquainted with Christianity and the religions of the East because there were quotations from various sacred writings. What struck him most was a line from the Old Testament, Eccles. 3: 11, "For God hath placed eternity in their hearts". This rang continuously in his ears during the hours of meditation. Was this the solution, to surrender oneself unconditionally to the eternity which we carry around with us in our own hearts? But shouldn't one then lose one's own self and be lost in the infinite? What self; the self of several years ago, of last year, this year or the self that is always changing in moods and phases of development? Can this limited, evasive and un-defined self after all be our real and eternal self?

Then it seemed as if a voice whispered to him, "He who loses his life, finds it. He who voluntarily gives up self finds his real self; not in isolation but in fellowship with the divine and with one's fellow men lies the solution."

He recognized the voice as well as the words; he had heard them spoken several times by the noblest man he had met in his life, Tenko Nishida.

As never before he realized that to cling to one's old self meant isolation, repression, bitter disappointment and death. What did it mean to let the eternity in our hearts come into its own? Could it mean that we lay ourselves open without reserve to the divine plan, tear down all barriers and become at one with all things living? There could no longer be any division between friend and enemy, relatives and strangers, foreigners and fellow country-men, male or female, educated and uneducated. Everything and everybody would belong to him who carries eternity in his heart. This was, so to speak, the first stage in the great experience Miao-Chi had on this unforgettable day of his conversion. Other experiences followed so that together they became a comprehensive synthesis which he had never before believed possible.

There was for instance the problem of the great dissonances in life, the tragic side of existence. These problems had tortured him throughout the years, but that day he was able to take up such intellectual crosses and regard them in the light of eternity.

How different they appeared! He saw the days and years on earth only as so many minutes and seconds, but important and precious minutes all the same during which much can be righted. But the real adjustment lay in the future. He saw how everything in life is a pilgrimage, and that the divine powers interpose and link the whole together so that not only is the law of retribution fulfilled but new possibilities for repentance, penance and renewal are created. What therefore becomes the great thing in life is that men should begin to see and think clearly. Through this comes wisdom, one of the most precious properties in the life of man. The tragedy of life is that most people have not obtained a glimpse of the basic pattern of life and have not discovered eternity within their own hearts. Thus they live as fools, and in the fires of lust and sensual craving work themselves deeper and deeper into complications. The best means of awakening them is by means of pain, suffering and bitter misfortune. Suffering and misfortune therefore assume in the light of eternity immense importance and become tranformed into great blessings. Still greater power and blessing lie in meeting good and holy men who have obtained enlightenment and have had their eyes of wisdom opened, men with merciful hearts and deep understanding.

How few there are of these men; not only among people in general but also among men of religion, among monks and priests, Buddhist literates and teachers of the law. All speak of a "pure and enlightened heart" and a "merciful disposition" but that often amounts to mere verbiage. Why? Because most of the monks and priests lead miserable lives of self-seeking. Their main interest centres itself upon personal advantage, promotion and comfort. Only short moments are dedicated to deep and sincere thinking and real care for others. Had it not also been true to a great extent with him? Had he in earnest decided to give himself to the service of mercy for others?

A feeling of shame and repentance passed through his mind.

Now it must and should become different. The aim of his life from this hour should be to lead as many as possible out of the darkness of ignorance and the sickness of self and to lighten as much as possible the burden of the world. He felt a stream of warmth and solemnity pass through him as he visualized a new and fruitful life in the service of wisdom and mercy. Now he knew why such a power of spirit and such a radiance was manifested in the life of his friend Tenko Nishida, who had given up his own former self and was living the life of eternity in the midst of time.

Here Miao-Chi reached the third stage; such a man, he could see, has nothing to fear when the body is broken by illness or old age. Death, the destruction of the body, eternity, all lay at once in a new light for Miao-Chi. He involuntarily smiled as he sat there. Fully aware of eternity in his inner self, willing to begin a new life in self-denial and love, he felt that he could go on as a pilgrim, strong, quiet, composed and joyful. Death, after all, is merely a move over from a worn-out, frail tent to a new and better dwelling. His real self, his liberated nature, his spirit would obtain a clothing or dwelling that would correspond to the stage of development reached.

He was led further and further in the spirit, and thus from stage to stage. The problems which had earlier oppressed him as heavy intellectual crosses now became clear and transparent. They fell harmoniously and easily into lines of thought and thus into unity as a complete, new and comprehensive outlook on life. Clarity, and with it peace, gently and reassuringly fell upon his mind, not as an intoxicating feeling but as a cool refreshment of soul. Everything rose to a level where even sorrow and evil could no longer spoil harmony. Without any thought of time and space he remained sitting when the leader gave the signal to disperse. The dinner bell sounded, the night bell too, and still he sat there. The others understood that his great hour had come, and nobody disturbed him. It was not until late into the night that he tore himself away to his cell. He felt no sense of fatigue or unhealthy reaction, only a deep calm peace that shone forth from his whole being and influenced others positively during the days that followed.

Miao-Chi's fellow monks and his superiors in the monastery soon noticed the change that had come over him. The same was true of Suzuki when, after some weeks, Miao-Chi came back after having finished his course. No one spoke much about it because in East Asia the rule that the book of Isaiah mentions holds good, "Over what is holy there is a cover".[1]

From now on, meditation claimed a predominant part in Miao-Chi's life. He could dispense with food and sleep but daily meditation, as quiet and as regular as possible, he could never do without. It was not that he always experienced something bordering upon ecstasy. That only happened now and then. He never sought to force this state, least of all by means of artificial yoga practices. Still, he obtained through his daily hours of meditation a deeper understanding of the interconnections of life. During these hours plans regarding his future work assumed a more definite shape in his mind. It had become much easier to "shut the door" and to enter into the sanctuary of his heart. Previously he had been dependent upon external conditions of peace; now he could enter into "his own self" wherever and whenever he wished, whether on train or tramcar or in the bustle of a big town.

[1] Isa. 4: 5.

BUDDHISM MAKES A MASTER

7

On China's Holy Island

IT WAS IN the early summer of 1920 that Miao-Chi saw China, the ancient soil of his ancestors, for the first time. His superiors in Formosa had agreed that he should have three years' study there: to visit the larger Buddhist centres of learning—Wuchang, Nanking and Amoy—to absorb as much as possible from the famous pilgrim centres and holy mountains, and meet some of the noted masters (*fa-shih*), and become acquainted with modern Buddhist publications.

His first visit was to P'u T'o Island, lying not far from Shanghai. It is one of the most important of the four Buddhist mountains to which, until recently, crowds of pilgrims used to stream in the season. The holy island, with its picturesque mountain top, is owned and administered by Buddhist monks. The sea tumbles fresh and blue against the cliffs and the open sandy beaches provide a fine bathing-place for people who desire an open-air life while fulfilling their obligations as pilgrims.

A number of monasteries and hundreds of minor hermitages and grottoes cover the mountain side. Of the monasteries two occupy prominent positions. The first stands near the landing-place, close to the little town where all the outfits for pilgrims are sold and where lodging-houses and restaurants are found. Its name is P'u Chi Ssu ("Monastery of Universal Salvation"). This building is of large dimensions and is famous for its architecture and furnishings. The great temple hall is impressive in size, and generous gifts from pilgrims have made it possible to use colossal sums on ornamentation and equipment.

Some distance inland, close to the ascent to Fu Ting ("Buddha Peak") lies the monastery which carries a significant name, Fa Yü Ssu ("Raining Law Monastery"). It seems even larger than its

sister monastery because of standing much higher and because so
many guest-rooms have been built in two complete storeys. Here
it is more peaceful than near the landing-place and that, of course,
is why many thoughtful Buddhists stay here because they shrink
from places unduly commercialized.

Miao-Chi too found a little cell in Fa Yü Ssu. He often took
walks on the island or along the steep path that winds up to
Buddha Peak. On the Peak has been erected a small lighthouse
which flashes its beam out to the vessels that ply across the Chusan
Archipelago. A small temple has been dug out of the south side of
the hill because the wind is so strong that it would be difficult for
an exposed house to remain standing. Miao-Chi, with his keen
sense of nature, could not see enough of the scenery visible to the
eye from this vantage point. Towards the east lay the China Sea.
To the north could be discerned the beautiful Chusan Islands.
Towards the west and south the mainland stood revealed as a
long grey-green strip, and behind lay the blue mountain ranges
of Chekiang Province. Miao-Chi's heart swelled at the thought of
how much this land had contained in spiritual values and greatness over many thousands of years. Here all the fine people who
had moulded the old Chinese civilization had lived their lives and
made their contribution. His own future work would be bound
up with the settlers in Formosa but he felt strongly the bond with
his own people. He felt it to be a great prospect that he would now
have not less than three years in the land of his ancestors. He felt
too that he had arrived in China as a renewed man. His aim therefore would be to serve his fellow men, to bring light and relief to
those who wandered in darkness and who endured inward fear
and pain.

China, he discovered, was not only a land of great memories; it
was also a land of dreadful suffering. On the one hand immense
wealth, accompanied by a refined mode of living and indulgence,
marked large sections of the town populations and upper classes;
on the other hand bottomless social needs among the lower classes
and in those districts that had been devastated by war, banditry
and corrupt administration. He had also noticed how among the
middle classes, industry, contentment and diligence were outstanding, and how large sections of the people, in spite of all their
misery and suffering, still preserved sound instincts of life.

Sometimes it seemed as if everybody and everything was

absorbed by toil and a desire for profit so that true religion tended to be excluded from life. He had observed worship in some of the Shanghai temples where people came and went during noisy performances, where salvoes of crackers exploded, where dice were thrown, where amid the electric lights spirals of smoke from incense sticks rose into dark clouds upon sooty walls. There seemed no devotion and no silence, only a bargaining devoid of spirituality and a chaffering with obscure deities. Even on P'u T'o Shan there were numerous worldly and often immoral monks who in the pilgrim season found good jobs for themselves. Great crowds of pilgrims too, drawn from all levels of society and from various levels of moral development, included many who were worthless.

Nevertheless many visitors came with sincerity to obtain religious understanding, consolation and peace for themselves and their dear ones who had passed away. This could be seen by their choice of lodging; they chose monasteries noted for pure and severe customs. It could be seen by their perseverance in worship. Instead of spending most of their time in playing cards or in aimless wandering through streets and alleys, they remained in the sanctuaries early and late. Not least it could be seen in their eagerness to hear venerable masters expound the scriptures and their desire to obtain personal help and spiritual guidance from monks who were noted for piety.

Miao-Chi knew that many of these sincere pilgrims had come from big cities along the coast of China and some from inland towns, and he observed with admiration their thoughtful charity. As a guest he was exempt from taking part in the huge masses for the pilgrims. His participation in the morning mass at three o'clock and his private meditations were sufficient. The rest of the time he could use for study, for conversation with teaching masters and for spiritual direction among the crowds of pilgrims. This became especially busy every week-end, because, in addition to the regular steamers from Ningpo, vessels from Shanghai brought floods of people. The largest guest-rooms in the temples were filled and a feverish rush began, ranging between worship in the sanctuaries and excursions to noted places. It was no wonder that some monks, particularly those who loved solitude, had built for themselves small huts on the Island, especially in mountain cliffs.

Miao-Chi went about from day to day among the crowds in order to seek for the sorrowing and the anxious. At the outset they were naturally somewhat non-committal, silent and reserved towards the strange monk who so generously distributed Buddhist tracts without wanting any payment. It was not long, however, before first one and then another felt that they could open their hearts to him, and the result was longer and deeper conversations. Connections and friendships were in several cases founded for life in those guest-rooms, and the vast correspondence which Miao-Chi later kept up, from the academy in Wuchang and during years of work on Formosa, had to a great extent its origin in P'u T'o in the summer of 1920.

An increasing number of monks also began to seek him. His frankness, scholarship and nobility of character attracted them; above all, here was a monk who cared for them. Even among monks there is often a lack of kindness, and many a lonely youth has suffered in silence in the monasteries. If there was any place where a person with the heart of a *bodhisattva* was needed it was just there. Among the monks he found good use for his insight into religious history; it was remarkable to see how many there were who hungered for a wider outlook.

8

Shanghai's Lay Buddhists

DURING THE SUMMER months on P'u T'o Island Miao-Chi met several of Shanghai's prominent Buddhist scholars and their families, and invitations awaited him from these friends and from some of the sanctuaries. Miao-Chi was very thankful for these invitations as he was interested in studying the Buddhist Lay Movement at close quarters. He had met on P'u T'o three scholars from Shanghai. They were a well-known triumvirate, Dr. Ting Fu-Pao, Mr. Wang Yi-T'ing and Mr. K'wong, long recognized as Buddhist lay leaders. Mr. Wang was a highly-educated man typical of old China, very rich and using his wealth for benefactions on a large scale among the poor and destitute in the city. He contributed large sums towards the restoration of temples and for the inauguration of social welfare institutions. He was an admirable scholar, landscape-painter and calligrapher, and it was considered a privilege to have his hand-written characters and signature on wall scrolls and paintings.

Mr. K'wong belonged to an old official family, and during many years as a magistrate had built up a large fortune, but had now come to an age when he felt he must prepare for eternity. He had become a leading figure in a laymen's temple in Shanghai and was connected with several philanthropic associations.

The most unusual of the trio, and the one with the most interesting history behind him, was a physician, Dr. Ting Fu-Pao, a small, active figure with beard trimmed in French fashion, radiant eyes and a courteous manner. In his youth he had studied medicine and by the age of thirty had become surgeon on one of China's first warships. In this post he remained for several years while his travels to the harbours and up the rivers of China widened his horizon and aesthetic sense. He became particularly interested in the pagodas and temples which blend so harmoniously in the river landscapes of China.

In one such temple he saw an attractive cast of Kuan-Yin. There she stood as Goddess of Mercy, surrounded by ocean spray and reaching out saving hands to those in distress. This figure so moved him that he made up his mind to begin a study of Buddhism. There was still no actual change of direction in his life, but an interest in religion had been awakened. A startling event was required before there could be conversion, and that event came. It happened one summer that Dr. Ting had just returned from a cruise in the China Seas and was going on short leave to his home district in the lower Yangtse. At Shanghai he boarded one of the small steamers which ply between the Yangtse ports and islands. As the vessel was leaving, everyone noticed that a storm was threatening. Those who have travelled in the Yangtse estuary know how the rapid current and a violent wind can create very rough water. As the wind increased, the position on board the overcrowded steamer soon became critical and shrill cries of fear arose from the passengers. The coastal population is well acquainted with the idea of Kuan-Yin as the special *bodhisattva* who assists those in trouble on the waters. Numbers began prostrating themselves on the deck, and in fear of their lives cried out, "O Kuan-Yin, thou *bodhisattva* of great mercy and compassion, save us! Save us!" Involuntarily Dr. Ting followed their example. He felt very unprepared and the fear of death contracted his heart. He promised himself that if only there could be a chance to begin life anew, oh! how different everything should be!

The storm increased to a typhoon, trees on the river bank were torn up by the roots, and the ship began to heel over, causing water to pour in upon the crowd of people. It was then that Ting Fu-Pao saw a vision; amid the water and spray on deck he discerned the figure which had previously made such an impression upon him—Kuan-Yin stood there with outstretched hands!

A superhuman power and a feeling of safety gripped him. He struggled over towards the windward side, and those nearest followed his example. Gradually the ship righted herself and was carried towards the river bank by wind and current. She was steered with difficulty into the mouth of a tributary and there anchored until the storm blew itself out. A few passengers had been washed overboard but the majority were safe.

This was the moment of conversion and renewal in Dr. Ting's life. He gave up his position as a naval surgeon and moved with his family to Shanghai where he began general practice. As soon as he was able to gather the necessary means together he started building a small temple at the mouth of the river. Over the altar there was set up a beautiful statue of Kuan-Yin.

Energetic, warm-hearted and eloquent, it was not long before Dr. Ting became prominent among Shanghai's lay Buddhists. Through the religious paper he started, the doctor influenced a great number of people. He wrote in a popular style and had an understanding not only of what would be of interest to the public but of the importance of scientific research. He attracted a number of able workers and with them undertook the editing of a greatly-enlarged and improved edition of the Chinese *Encyclopedia of Buddhist Terms and Expressions*. It was not only with Buddhism that he occupied himself; some of the treasures of Taoism and Confucianism were included in his literary scope. Dr. Ting's bookshop in Bubblingwell Road came to be regarded as the best in the country for Chinese religious literature. After his own experience of the power of religion he felt too the urgency of emphasizing to sick folk that the day of miracles was far from past. He never wearied of emphasizing that Kuan-Yin, as omni-present and ever-merciful spirit, stood ready to help where medicine and doctors were useless.

At the layman's temple in the densely-populated Chapei district of Shanghai the doctor introduced Miao-Chi when they returned together from P'u T'o Island. The temple itself was old and by no means beautiful but it was arranged in a practical manner, and the stimulating personality of Dr. Ting contributed much to lay Buddhists there. Many of these were business men who, as often as possible, tore themselves free to spend a few days' quiet together in the common home. The temple hall is large and so is the lecture-hall facing the street, where open-air preaching often takes place, as in Christian practice, with a harmonium, choir, witness-ing and choruses. The main sanctuary is a small annexe on the roof where there has been set up a precious *shê-li* ("relic pearl") in which the essential spiritual and physical substance of a holy man is believed to be crystallized. The sanctuary walls are constructed of plate glass and illuminated by electric light. An extraordinary brightness and radiance can thereby spread over the whole room.

In this place Miao-Chi was glad to have an opportunity of meeting numbers of truly religious people.

Miao-Chi's stay at another lay temple situated in the west end of the city proved of even greater interest. It is called Chin Nieh Shê ("Society for Accumulation of Merit"), and stands in Hart Road, a comparatively quiet district. This temple, of more recent date, is connected with the modern renascence within Chinese Buddhism and closely reflects the Lay Movement in Shanghai.

In the temple hall stand three gilded figures of "perfected Buddhas"; Sakyamuni in the centre, Bhaisajyaguru, the great physician, to the right, and Amitabha to the left. From an artistic viewpoint this is one of the most outstanding groups executed in China in modern times. The Apollo type, so well known from Graeco-Scythian times, has been blended with ancient Chinese art and the ideal of Buddhism. Perfect wisdom and harmony and all-embracing mercy are revealed in the faces.

Miao-Chi felt it to be a real privilege to move into the temple belonging to the Society for the Accumulation of Merit. Many leading monks gathered here in order to confer with the Buddhist literati, and there were famous Buddhist masters who continually lectured on important *sutras*. He had frequent opportunity for profound and enlightening conversations with such leaders.

Lectures were given every afternoon from two o'clock, and a number of better-class Chinese, both men and women, solemnly gathered to hear the exposition of one *sutra* or another. All possessed copies of the *sutra* in question and some brought notebooks and pencils too. After a short act of devotion the *fa-shih* mounted the rostrum and seated himself. As a rule two and a half hours elapsed before he descended. Another short hymn of devotion and then they dispersed.

The most solemn gatherings were on Sundays. Large numbers of lay Buddhists gathered as soon as they had finished their breakfast and remained at the temple throughout the day. After a long morning devotion a procession was formed through the corridors and garden. Hundreds of men and women took part, led by monks, and a subdued murmur rose and fell from many throats, always the same, the well-known formula, "Nan-wu, O-mi-t'o-fu!"[1]

Most of them knew the secret of the constant repetition of the

---

[1] "I trust thee, Amitabha!"

holy name, and many who had not learned it were soon suggest-
ively uplifted into a mystical experience. They realized gradually
that if they called upon the name with concentrated mind and
sincere faith they were led into a peaceful haven, or were lifted
up to a new level where everything takes on a different aspect
from how it is experienced during the greyness of daily life. Or
again, it meant entrance into a new world where an undreamed
of future and peace opened up. Truly this is auto-suggestion and
religious mass-suggestion put into effect.

At noon there was a break of about three hours. Tables were
laid with a simple meal of rice, vegetables and various forms of
soya beancurd. This break was used for conversation and social
intercourse. People gathered in small groups in the guest-room
and smaller rooms or sat together in pavilions, in grottoes by the
pools or under shady trees, and there exchanged thoughts and
shared experiences from life. A constant noise of traffic rose from
the street outside but the groups that sat together did not appear
to notice it. Again the drum sounded as a signal for gathering in
the temple hall. Muffled strokes on the "wooden fish"[1] announced
that all was ready, and then a monk intoned the first verse of a
hymn of praise, "O mysterious depths (of wisdom and purity)!
O omnipresent and active! O immovable prince of perfect
wisdom and harmony! Of thy like truly there are but few on
earth!" Then the others joined in with a mighty chorus, "I pray
thee to blot out all those shifting and vain lusts that I have carried
with me through innumerable *kalpas* (long periods of time), so
that I may not have to wander through limitless aeons before I
sense my true essence of life (*dharma-kaya*). Now I vow to bear
fruit and realize my ideal as a prince of the spirit world. I vow to
share in the salvation of all living beings, numerous as the sand of
the Ganges. I prostrate myself and pray. May the world-honoured
one be my witness; if I do not first help all creation to obtain
Buddhahood then may I myself never attain perfection. Hail!
O eternal Buddha! In all the world, hail, O Sakyamuni Buddha!"

When all was finished the procession re-formed and returned
along the same route through the garden and corridors. Again
the "Nan-wu, O-mi-t'o-fu" was heard, showing that the Pure

[1] The "wooden fish" is a hollowed-out piece of wood in the shape of a fish's head. By
tapping this object Buddhist monks and laymen are given the time for chanting the
sutras, whether fast or slow. The fish is the symbol of perpetual watchfulness because "the
fish never sleeps".

D

Land attitude was dominant; only one thing was required, a faithful invocation.

When such a procession began, one section of lay Buddhists always stood aristocratically aloof. This was a group of literary men from superior levels of society who had taken up the so-called Wei Shih philosophy for special study. The Wei Shih School (Sanscrit, *Yogachara*) is highly speculative. It is often called the Idealistic School because it stresses that behind shifting phenomena and events there lies continuity. The School is sometimes called intellectual since adoration plays little or no part, whereas meditative speculations and dialogues between individuals under the guidance of a Wei Shih master are encouraged. In Shanghai the Wei Shih School exercised some influence, and a room in the top storey of the lay temple had been handed over to them and was well frequented, especially on Sundays.

Many of these gentlemen had long conversations with Miao-Chi, and they were struck by his psychological insight. They asked him to come up and join the select circle in the tower room but Miao-Chi did not feel happy there. Among several sincere and moderate members there was a distressing number of parrots and boasters who held the floor continuously in order to show off their philosophical knowledge. The consequence was that such gatherings were chilly. How different it was down below! In spite of that simple and naïve calling upon the name of Amitabha, one thing was certain; warm-heartedness and sincerity lay behind it.

9

Meditation on the "Golden Mount"

MIAO-CHI BEGAN HIS travel up the Yangtse Valley by taking
the train from Shanghai to Chinkiang, where a noted monastery
of the Meditation School stood on a small peninsula jutting out
into the Yangtse. It was called Chin Shan Ssu ("Golden Mount
Monastery").[1]

Here courses in meditation were given lasting from three
months to three years. To have gone through such a course gave a
monk great advantage and secured for him quick promotion.
Numerous monks, however, recoiled in fear from undertaking a
complete course as it made almost superhuman demands upon
endurance. In addition to long acts of devotion from two until
five every morning, and equally long hours in the afternoon, the
course divided day and night into periods of meditation, inter-
rupted only by two meals, one hour of sleep and one hour for
washing clothes. Many candidates made their escape after a
couple of weeks. Those who endured were reckoned to have
accumulated great merit and to be fit for the highest positions.

Miao-Chi resolved to take the short three months' course. He
settled down in the meditation hall, which served at the same time
as a dormitory during the short time set aside for sleep. A wide
shelf along the walls provided both bed and seat. Above, another
shelf provided a little space for clothes and other possessions.
A nameplate marked the restricted space at the disposal of each
individual.

Strokes on the "wooden fish" indicated that a period of meditation, for three full hours, was about to begin. The period

[1] In February, 1948, this famous monastery was burnt to the ground. During the fire
twenty of the older monks shut themselves inside the temple hall and continued mass until
they were consumed in the flames. The abbot, who had been brought out earlier, had to be
held back by force from joining the group which, through this "purging fire", hoped to
enter Nirvana.

opens with a rapid march around the altar standing apart in the centre. From a march the tempo increases to a run and then to what appears to be a wild rush. The speed is directed by the instructor and his assistant who are equipped with long bamboo poles. Several young monks carry a small flat ruler. With this they give the man in front a series of sharp blows between the shoulder blades. It is said that this sets the blood circulating properly! After a while the speed is relaxed and at a signal from the stick everyone goes to his place and sits down cross-legged, his monk's robes folded underneath as a cushion.

Then follows a short instruction, such as, "It is important to remember that we are gathered in the real sanctuary of Buddhism, more holy and important than the temple hall with its Buddha images. The temple hall is only an ante-chamber where one can read masses and worship. Here all thought of prayer and worship of a Buddha outside oneself is to be banished. Buddha and Amitabha are indeed one's own self in its highest unfolding and development. It is important to scrutinize the self. Therein lies deliverance. It is necessary to penetrate to one's own original countenance, which is one with all life. There is found the basic pattern of life, of which all people carry a darkened reflection within them. This reflection must become clear and radiant. The false ego must be blotted out, for it is unreal and transient, connected as it is with matter."

The instructor then proceeds to give a vivid description of the false ego, bordering upon the repulsive, and concludes, "Even the strongest and most handsome person carries with him this corpse of uncleanness. Sooner or later the end will come in sickness, age and death. It is therefore important to emerge from illusion and escape from decay and corruption." Again the chief instructor strikes the "wooden fish" and complete stillness reigns. Not a limb moves. Now and then someone coughs and spits. There are no spittoons. The sole of a thick shoe rubs the floor and that is all. Thus are the demands of hygiene fulfilled! The floor is never washed but merely swept. It is easy to imagine what such a floor is like after hundreds of monks have finished their violent exercise. No wonder Chin Shan Ssu was one of the most notorious places for developing tuberculosis.

Miao-Chi had had experience of meditation monasteries in Japan which were clean and well run. Here everything was different; airless and dusty buildings, inadequate food and a plan of work so one-sided and exacting that even the strongest constitutions suffered. Miao-Chi had a will of iron; what he felt to be his duty he willingly undertook even if it meant considerable exertion. He did not need to bother over expositions from the instructor, for he had found a higher and better way of thinking.

After a couple of months there came an opportunity to obtain a week's breathing space, as a major repair had to be carried out in the meditation hall. Miao-Chi decided to make closer acquaintance with the monastery buildings and neighbourhood. The most notable building at that time was the mighty pagoda standing on the hill top. By climbing the spiral stair to the top a magnificent view could be obtained over the Yangtse and Grand Canal. On festival days the pagoda used to be visited by thousands of people. They came partly for the view and partly because for pilgrims to climb such a holy place as a pagoda is reckoned to accumulate great merit. Under most pagodas there lies a sacred relic.

Miao-Chi saw Chiao Shan Island far out in the Yangtse and decided to make a trip there because he had heard much about Chiao Shan's choral masses.

On approaching Chiao Shan the forest shows up green and dense, and it is soon obvious that large flocks of birds have settled there. These are mostly local birds but the island is also a regular stopping-place for migrants; consequently there is always a great singing and twittering going on. Is it that which makes the monks on Chiao Shan so famous for their choral masses? No monk is received into either of the Chiao Shan monasteries unless he has a specially good voice and musical ear. Consequently the most beautiful sung masses resound over the Yangtse at night-time and in the late afternoon. It is during the afternoon services that something unique can be heard; flocks of birds appear to be attracted by the singing, and they mingle their trilling and whistling with the temple chorus. It is mildly astonishing, for the result is not entirely harmonious. The sung mass of the monks is always full of sadness and in a minor key; the flocks of birds, on the contrary, exult in a jubilant major.

On the last day of the holiday Miao-Chi visited some of the hermits who spent their meditation time in private cells and in small straw huts near Chin Shan Monastery. These monks never took part in public worship nor came to meals. They fetched their food from the common kitchen but otherwise very seldom left their cells. A bed, a table, a bench to sit on and a little altar with a Buddha image made up the entire furnishing. Sometimes the altar and image were lacking and only a small shelf, with a couple of important scriptures folded in a piece of fine cloth, denoted the place of an altar. Sometimes the cell was so small that it only allowed space for a few planks, where the bedding was spread out.

Several of these hermits were of forbidding appearance, with overgrown hair and beard and attired in monkish garb made up from multi-coloured rags. Many of them did not answer when Miao-Chi tried to open conversation with them, having taken a vow of silence. Others, on the contrary, were affable. This was especially the case with two lamas, one a Mongol and the other a Tibetan, who had already spent several years there. They spoke enthusiastically of their lama brotherhood which extends across the political boundaries of Central Asia, from Manchuria in the East and far into Russian territories in the West. They themselves had travelled on foot over vast mountain ranges and worshipped at all the sacred places. They therefore felt safely assured of a glorious reincarnation whenever they should leave this existence and continue upon their great journey. Miao-Chi felt rather troubled on hearing this, because he realized that the whole foundation of such thinking was frail and uncertain.

10

The Ascetics of "Precious Flower"

HAVING FINISHED HIS course at "Golden Mount", Miao-Chi went on to nearby Pao Hua Shan ("Precious Flower Mountain"), not far from Nanking. This monastery had become the centre of the Law School and one of the main centres for the ordination of monks. Twice a year, in autumn and spring, these ordinations take place and large crowds of men and women come from far and near to take part in the course of three months' instruction as well as in the ceremonies of ordination. The majority proceed to complete ordination which leads up to the full profession of monk or nun. There are also considerable numbers who cannot break loose from their homes and who content themselves with *shou-wu-chai-ti* (ordination of the five commandments). That is, they undertake to observe the five cardinal commandments which are: (1) not to take life, i.e. to live as vegetarians, (2) not to tell lies, (3) not to steal, (4) not to commit adultery, (5) not to indulge in intoxicating drinks. Such people are given a special garb but they are permitted to wear ordinary dress while engaged in everyday tasks.

Miao-Chi's visit to Pao Hua Shan coincided with the ordination ceremonies of the autumn term. The vast compound seethed with monks and nuns, and extra dining-rooms were required for meals. For such occasions extra monks are called in from neighbouring monasteries. These act as instructors and exert a despotic authority with their bamboo sticks. As it is impossible to gather all the people together in one place the temple courtyard is used as a meeting place for instruction classes. Here also a part of the ordination ceremony takes place but the most sacred act, that of consecration, takes place on the sacred *chai-t'ai* (platform of consecration), surrounded by selected elders, among whom the confessor and chief instructor occupy places of importance. The abbot receives the ordinands two at a time and in a low and solemn voice consecrates and blesses them. This act is reckoned to confer holy succession upon monks and nuns. Afterwards follows the consecration to Buddhahood when the ordinands undertake their obligation to share in the great work of "saving all living creatures." The burning of "Buddha's marks" upon each head follows as the last act.

In order to emphasize that the buildings are the centre of the severe and puritanical School of Law, the buildings of Pao Hua Shan are as simple as possible, but remnants of old walls dating back to A.D. 1200 and stone slabs still show marks of ancient greatness and exquisite taste. Most famous, perhaps, is the immense ordination platform constructed of fine granite with many finely-carved decorations. The form of the monastery is somewhat peculiar, as it has been modelled upon a lotus flower in full bloom, but the characteristic lines of a classical monastery are also evident.

The whole life at Pao Hua Shan also seems to be cast in an austere mould. It is to be seen in the garb of the monks, the cloth being coarse and rough and the colour a rusty brown or black. Food is of the simplest kind. The rule is that only two meals are served, one at five or six in the morning and another about eleven. In the afternoon nothing may be consumed except water or tea. However, nature sometimes overrules discipline so that some manage an afternoon snack, such as noodles, that goes under the name of "lighter meal".

There is, however, a group of decided ascetics who live according to the letter of the law. They are to be seen with their eyes cast down in order to watch lest they should involuntarily tread on even the tiniest creeping thing. Amongst these monks a number are not content with the marks of branding at their consecration. From time to time, often on the anniversary of their ordination or on Buddha's birthday, they burn in new marks on their arms or chest, or burn off a whole finger joint or cut out a piece of muscle from an arm.

Miao-Chi met a monk on Pao Hua Shan who had recently burnt in a complete rosary around his neck and down to the region of his stomach with the Chinese character for Buddha in the centre. This monk was in a pitiful state because the wounds had become infected, and it was apparently almost as bad with another monk who had fastened two large iron hooks into the muscles of his chest. At certain times he hung two iron chains on the hooks and these he dragged around with him on his walks. Shaken at the sight, Miao-Chi gave these two monks a long talk on the meaninglessness of such mortification. He pointed out how it resulted from a superficial and wrong understanding of the *Lotus Sutra* and other sacred writings where this kind of self-castigation appears to be indicated. The meaning of the scripture actually is that one should be willing to undergo all kinds of privation and sufferings if one can thereby help people and do honour to the name of Buddha. The monk with the "rosary" listened attentively but the ascetic with the iron chains hastened away. Miao-Chi soon discovered the motives involved; the former had undergone the self-torture in the hope of obtaining spiritual help, the latter merely sought to awake compassion and thereby earn money. He only wore his chains when pilgrims were watching!

Yuan-Kuang, the monk with the "rosary", felt overcome by the solicitude which Miao-Chi showed towards him and threw himself on his face exclaiming, "It has never happened before that any monk has shown me any kindness. To-day you have shown me compassion!" Then he recounted how he had lived as a hermit up on the heights of Pao Hua Shan where a few ascetics live in caves or straw huts, of how he had for several years wandered along the pilgrim routes from his home province in Szechuan to visit sacred mountains in Yunnan and Shansi, and how recently he had been at P'u T'o on the coast.

Like many others, Yuan-Kuang was enmeshed in a net of superstition. Restless in mind he went from place to place hoping to meet a good master who would show him the way, but so far had been bitterly disappointed. No one cared for him; uneducated and poor as he was, the only way now open to him was to undertake an act of self-torture which would secure for him at one stroke great and lasting merit.

One of the hermits up on the heights had come to his aid, and with a firm hand had sketched the long rosary around his neck and upon his thin and emaciated body. He had helped him too with the remaining act. Slowly and firmly he let a spill of burning paper move along the outlines until the whole rosary and the character for Buddha were burnt in. Yuan-Kuang stood up bravely to the ordeal. By continuously reciting, "O-mi-t'o-fu!"

he had tried to conjure away the pain, but when the painful operation was at last over he had fainted and his assistant had had to prepare strong tea in order to bring him round. However, he was so tough that by the next day he was able to go down to the monastery for his food. Here it was that Miao-Chi met him. His suffering was still intense but a glow of ascetism shone from his agonized face. "Come and visit me in my hut to-morrow!" he implored. Miao-Chi promised and next morning he was there. He found Yuan-Kuang lying in a high fever as a result of his burns and babbling deliriously. Miao-Chi's first task was that of nurse. Day after day he went up to Yuan-Kuang's hut, applied bandages to the painful burns, boiled rice gruel and gave the patient strengthening herbal medicine.

The hut was dark and untidy so Miao-Chi set about cleaning it. In the monastery he managed to borrow some carpenter's tools and soon he had constructed a window with a wooden lattice. From the bed two staring eyes followed Miao-Chi's movements but for days not a word was exchanged between them. Yuan-Kuang was in a state of feverish delirium, but one morning he woke up. His first words upon seeing Miao-Chi were significant. "You are a true *bodhisattva* sent from heaven. I have never met anyone like you. Oh, if you would only receive me as your disciple!"

His recovery was rapid and the two friends were able to converse in earnest. Miao-Chi gave him of his best and Yuan-Kuang took it all in eagerly. He persisted until Miao-Chi agreed to accept him as his disciple. They could not, of course, always be together but they could maintain correspondence.

At the beginning of November Miao-Chi had to leave Pao Hua Shan in order to move on to Nanking. He had taken leave of Yuan-Kuang the evening before as he was due to leave at day-break. In the morning he looked for the carrier who was to help him with his belongings, but another man stood waiting instead; it was Yuan-Kuang who stood ready with a carrying-pole. He wanted to perform a service for his master.

11

Nanking's Philosophers

MIAO-CHI'S MAIN PURPOSE in visiting Nanking was to attend a course at the Lay Buddhist Academy situated in the centre of the city. The day he arrived he found himself surrounded by a picked group of scholarly monks, Buddhist scholars and prominent *fa-shih*. This Chinese Academy for Deeper Studies has an interesting history.

One of China's scholars, Yang Wen-Hui, who had long served in the country's diplomatic service, and who had spent many years in America and Europe, was sent in 1875 to Japan as Chinese Ambassador. He was deeply interested in religious matters and used all his leisure to study Japanese Buddhism. Yang Wen-Hui belonged to a family of officials noted for Buddhist interests and he too found his spiritual home in that religion. At the same time he had adopted many ideas from other higher religions, notably from Christianity. During his stay in Japan he studied specially those schools and tendencies which were either wholly extinct or of little importance in China. These included primarily the Idealistic School and the School of Mystery. When he returned to his ancestral home in Nanking Yang Wen-Hui resolved to retire from official life and devote himself wholly to the study of religion. He set aside a large part of his home, with its park and pavilions, for Buddhist scholars and monks of high standing to gather for study and deliberation. In this way the nucleus was formed of the first Buddhist layman's academy in China. The Yang family set aside a considerable sum of money too for the maintenance of the Academy. In the autumn of 1880 it was officially opened. The first course had twelve students, seven scholars and five monks. Students were accepted only after careful sifting and upon recommendations from well-known men.

The whole arrangement of the Academy was different from the monastic schools. In the centre stood the administrative building with a common refectory, reception hall and dining-rooms. Yang himself lived in the upper storey, together with his secretaries and assistant teachers. The students had accommodation in pavilions which had been altered into studies and bedrooms. Another large house had been converted into a library and temple hall. This hall was small and simply furnished. Over the little altar was enthroned a white marble statue of Sakyamuni Buddha, with golden decorations and inlaid with jade and precious stones. The statue came from Burma. Apart from this one there were no statues to be seen but the walls were richly decorated with artistic scrolls and quotations from Buddhist literature.

At the outset regular devotions were held morning and evening conducted by the monks. Later, such devotions were limited to special occasions, whereas meditation was held in high honour, not as compulsory for all but as a private exercise in the cells of individuals. It was during these quiet hours that students were expected to reach the main goal of the Academy, an understanding of the secrets of the Idealistic School, i.e. Wei Shih philosophy.

Yang always maintained in his lectures that each of the Buddhist schools had its own significance because of meeting the various spiritual needs of the human soul. Whenever he spoke of this he became eloquent. He often used to mention his experiences during a stay in Christian lands where he had noticed how many Christians felt uplifted by the singing of hymns in powerful evangelistic meetings. Others he noticed preferred quiet and pointed sermons that appealed to the intellect. Others too gathered around the mystical and the sacramental, attracted by richly-suggestive ritual and dignified ceremonial. "For my own part," he said, "I can benefit from taking part in the worship of various schools, for they lead, each in their own way, into the sanctuary of 'the unspeakable' where men obtain a glimpse of the true pattern of life. Nevertheless I feel that the most direct way for me personally is the Wei Shih philosophy."

This outspoken tolerance and spiritual breadth of Yang were revealed further in his relationships with Christian missionaries. He greatly enjoyed conversation upon religious subjects with men like Timothy Richard and David Hill. He tirelessly assisted Dr. Richard in his attempt to translate some of the Buddhist texts into English. No wonder that Yang's pupils became attached to him. After five or six years Wei Shih Societies began to spring up as Yang's group of students spread through the land. When he died in 1912 a large number gathered at his funeral in Nanking to show their respect and gratitude. Yang had appointed as his successor Ou-Yang Ching Wu, one of his dearest and most promising disciples, who later became a famous scholar.

Miao-Chi was accepted for a two months' course at Ou-Yang's Academy, and he gradually succeeded during this period in comprehending the viewpoint of the Idealistic School. Ou-Yang soon realized that here was a student who, to a rare degree, possessed the mental capacity for a full understanding of modern Buddhist philosophy. During his first conversation with Miao-Chi he presented him with a copy of his own most important work, *Buddhism, neither Religion nor Philosophy*. The conclusion at which Ou-Yang had arrived was summarized as follows: "Buddhism rightly understood is simply finding the way of life and the meaning of life. In other words, Buddhism is the right wisdom of life."

Western historians of religion have agreed to call the movement the Idealist School. "Idealist" is here understood as a tendency towards continuity exclusively related to individuals. The highly-compressed Chinese term agrees with this designation because the words "*wei-shih*", when analysed, mean "mere observation", i.e. everything depends upon subjective observation and perception. Opposition to materialist ways of thought comes particularly to the fore in this Chinese term, for materialism is in Chinese called "*wei-wu-lun*", i.e. "nothing but matter exists".

If the lines of thought in this Wei Shih School are examined more closely one comes first to the eight categories of consciousness.

The first five are derived from the senses; sight, hearing, smell, taste and somatic feeling. These senses man has in common with the animal world, but peculiar to man are three more developed faculties. The sixth category is the faculty of thinking. From this is developed the seventh, the *mona* faculty which discriminates between man as an "ego being" and all that lies outside. Conscious life begins here. Most important, perhaps, is the eighth category called *olaya vijnana*. This rather obscure term can best be translated "store of consciousness" or "total consciousness".

Vasubandhu[1] insisted that what is peculiar to man as an individual is that a "store" is created in his life-stream out of constantly-changing and vanishing events. Much slips away from the conscious mind but is gathered in the subconscious. One's *olaya* becomes an expression for both the life of the heart and the subconscious and conscious life. Through his *olaya* man is tied to the pulsating life of the universe. The changing picture of events and experiences which men conceive and form for themselves becomes their world. Apart from this picture men cannot know the universe. Thus the world of one person is different from that of another. The difference is dependent upon how a man has developed the life of his senses, his intellect and thinking and his particular self-consciousness. If he has developed a well-planned ethical life of kindness there is developed a correspondingly harmonious and good *olaya* (inner life). If he has let the senses have unbridled course there will necessarily be developed a correspondingly evil, disharmonious and suffering inner life. In other words, *olaya* becomes one's heaven or hell!

If the Wei Shih philosophy be studied further it will soon be found that it tends to follow the same lines as traditional Buddhism, especially as clearly determined by the writings of the T'ien T'ai and Ch'an Schools. For example, the *olaya* hypothesis presumes reincarnation quite clearly. The only difference is that more stress is laid on the personal "store" which continues to operate in one's life. In other words, more is spoken of continuity; not that the soul continues its life (for the Wei Shih viewpoint denies the idea of an everlasting soul), but a certain personal life, as a basis for mental activity, continues. It has become very common in this School to juggle with the obscure term "mental essence". It is argued that physical death cannot bring any change other than a stronger accentuation of suffering or progress. Salvation consists in arriving at an understanding of the right way to conduct one's life. This cannot be found by looking outward, for there one sees merely kaleidoscopic picures. Further, man's senses are utterly deceptive, and both the observer and what is seen are constantly changing; we and the world-picture necessarily change not only every day but every minute. It becomes necessary therefore to turn mind and thought inwards. A man

---

[1] One of the Indian twin founders of the Yogachara School (Chinese, Wei Shih School) of Buddhism. Approximately second century A.D.

must leave not only the external and deceptive interplay of the life of the senses but keep away from the "inner thief", i.e. ordinary thinking determined by the senses. By concentration and meditation he can rise to an elevated level of intuition and contemplation in which there begins a realization of his original nature in its connection with the life of the universe.

It can be understood that this form of Buddhism is calculated to impress those whose interest is modern and rationalistic. In its moral and psychological aspect the movement has helped many believers to take their stand against the superstition that mars so many sections of Buddhism. Yet it can be seen that the Wei Shih movement has in many ways weakened and diluted the already thin religious enthusiasm amongst educated classes in East Asia. Indeed it is a well-known fact that the Wei Shih School, in spite of many relatively sound psychological and moral ideas, is the least religious of all the Buddhist schools, for there is no movement that so clearly and decidedly leaves out the living God. In many places the Wei Shih School has sunk to the level of little more than mental hygiene.

Buddhism, whether Hinayana or Mahayana, must undoubtedly be characterized as a religion. Now the Wei Shih School is obviously the least religious of the Buddhist schools, for pure thought and logic have predominated to such an extent as to dilute considerably the element of awe as well as that of the holy. This judgment the author has heard expressed by Chinese Buddhists who are outstanding in scholarship and clarity of thought as well as in warmth and depth of feeling. This was Miao-Chi's impression too after concluding his course of study in the Nanking Academy. His remark about it is significant: "The only point where the Wei Shih School touches pure religion is in mention of Nirvana. Here pure thinking and strict logic have come to an end, and one has to talk about 'the unspeakable' and 'majestic loftiness', vague ideas that only a 'perfected Buddha' can fully comprehend."

Miao-Chi felt it quite a relief at the end of his two months' course to move among people for whom religion meant something more than psychological training and mental hygiene. His travels now led him further up the Yangtse to another famous centre, Chiu Hua Shan.

12

Pilgrims to "Nine Flowery Peaks"

CHIU HUA SHAN ("Nine Flowery Mountains", a reference to the number of peaks) is situated in the Yangtse valley not far from the town of Tatung. It is one of the Ssu Ta Ming Shan ("Four Famous Mountains") which the majority of Buddhist monks hope to visit at least once in a lifetime—P'u T'o, Chiu Hua, Wu T'ai and Omei.

Chiu Hua Shan is about three thousand feet high and is perhaps the most delightful of the four classic mountains. It cannot compare with Omei Shan in majestic splendour, nor with P'u T'o Island for its peculiar solemnity, but because it is so central and easily accessible it is a favourite meeting-place for pilgrims, surrounded as it is by beautiful valleys and flower-covered hillsides.

Even between seasons one frequently meets visitors up there, especially at the winter and spring ordinations. Miao-Chi's visit occurred during winter. He had met a number of pilgrims already on the river steamer. The yellow sashes over their breasts were marked with the character *t'u* (earth) indicating that their goal was Chiu Hua Shan. Its guardian genius is the merciful *bodhisattva* Ti-Ts'ang (Sanscrit, *Kitsigarbha*) who, according to Chinese tradition, went down into the depths to fulfil his vow not to leave the Kingdom of Death before its last prisoner has been brought over the ocean of sorrow to Nirvana. It is said that Ti-Ts'ang broke into the torture chambers of hell and there preached the law of salvation to distressed spirits. He is often depicted holding a key and a shining jewel in his hand symbolizing that he alone has the key of the Kingdom of Death and can lead the wretched out of utter darkness by the light of his jewel.

According to tradition Ti-Ts'ang became incarnate in Korea (others say in Thailand) during the T'ang dynasty in the year

A.D. 730. He was, like Sakyamuni, a prince but voluntarily renounced the position. During his wanderings in China he reached the neighbourhood of Chiu Hua Shan accompanied by his faithful white dog. Finding the place auspicious he settled down on one of the nine flowery peaks and lived there in solitude until his death at the age of ninety-nine. Local people noticed strange lights on the mountain peak and these lights eventually turned into flames. It was then understood that something unusual had happened to the hermit who spent his time there in meditation. His body was found on the mountain top and buried nearby where Chiu Hua Shan's mighty pagoda now stands. It was revealed that the holy man was no other than Buddha himself and that he had in this way become incarnate to prepare for the work of preaching in Hades.

Several of the pilgrims whom Miao-Chi met on the steamer were mourning the loss of relatives. Pilgrims are always reticent when fulfilling the vow of visiting a holy place as it is believed that to secure the best result their minds must be collected and pure. Thus it was not easy for Miao-Chi to converse with them. That he was a Buddhist helped a good deal of course, especially when travellers experienced his kindness. After a while small groups of pilgrims gathered around him and Miao-Chi used the opportunity to give to each individual a word of comfort and exhortation. He spoke of the significance of sorrow and how it could help people as nothing else to gather their thoughts and concentrate on real and eternal values. Numbers grew and when Tatung was reached the following evening many pilgrims implored him to join their company.

To get ashore from a Yangtse River steamer at night is sometimes an adventurous experience. With loud shouts a long rope is thrown as the ferry glides in towards the side of the moving steamer. Passengers aboard the ferry fall backwards as a result of the tremendous jerk when the rope suddenly becomes taut. Amid continuous shouting and clatter all kinds of objects are thrown down into the boat—bundles of bedding, well-filled baskets covered with netting, bags and boxes. At the same time the people who want to get ashore press forward and jump headlong down into the boat. If one or two fall into the water and disappear this is not taken too seriously. Anyhow rescue is out of the question in that swirling current, and if someone is drowned

E

that must have been predestined by higher powers, or a malicious demon saw its chance to get a fresh human soul into his clutches! Then the ferry casts off and travels rapidly down stream until it is finally rowed into the mouth of the river where Tatung is situated.

It was late at night when Miao-Chi came ashore into streets badly lighted with oil lamps, but in between there were places where torches were burning and where life went on as busily as in the daytime. This was the hotel district that did a specially good trade in the pilgrim season. Pennants with high-faluting inscriptions waved here and there. In the streets were "runners" with printed cards to tell pilgrims about the advantages of accommodation in this or that hotel, "the most exquisite vegetarian food", "excellent incense from the Province of Fukien", "temporary altars erected for devotion", and so on.

Miao-Chi and his company entered one of these hostels, not to sleep but in order to wait quietly for the dawn. While breakfast was being prepared the pilgrims held their morning devotions. Kneeling-mats of thick straw were laid out in the courtyard. Incense was lighted and a leader took his place at the altar provided. In long familiar style he intoned prayers to Amitabha and Ti-Ts'ang. The others joined in at intervals with the refrain, "O Ti-Ts'ang *bodhisattva*! In awe we bring incense to thy holy mountain. Have mercy upon us!" Then followed more prayers by the leader, "O merciful Amitabha, thou who didst undertake forty-eight vows of grace, have mercy upon us!", "O merciful Kuan-Yin *p'usa*,[1] thou who revealest thyself in thirty-two diverse manifestations, have mercy upon us!" "O merciful Ti-Ts'ang *p'usa*, thou who hast promised not to leave the Kingdom of Death until the last have been released, have mercy upon us!"

At daybreak breakfast was eaten, consisting of rice gruel and a dish of vegetables. Some had brought small bags of rice with them but most bought a little rice at the inn. During its preparation it was closely watched lest a scrap of animal fat be added to the vegetables; only a little vegetable oil and salt could be used. Some carried a small pot with them fearing that the one used in the inn had been polluted earlier by animal fat. Then incense-sticks were lighted and with these in their hands the procession began to move forward. At certain intervals the prayer refrains were repeated.

[1] *p'usa* is the Chinese form of *bodhisattva*.

Miao-Chi kept in the rear. He carried his bedding and other belongings on a carrying-pole. About nine o'clock they rested for a while in order to drink tea, re-adjust their sandals and light fresh incense-sticks. The longest pause was at noon when another meal was taken and a longer period of worship was observed. Certain pilgrims took it even more seriously. Some had taken a vow to stop at every twentieth or fiftieth pace when they threw themselves on the ground while chanting the prayer refrain. This of course meant considerable delay but the "merit" gained was all the greater.

Miao-Chi had long ago considered this question of "merit", and had come to the conclusion that external austerity could at the best have significance in the training of the will. The danger of externalism lay perilously near because all this could easily lead people into self-delusion. He spoke about this in the evening when his group halted for the night, and several in the company gave him their approval. The inn was crowded. Several bands of pilgrims had returned from the mountain worn and exhausted but in their eyes shone a fanatical fire. An evening mass was held simultaneously by all these groups in front of temporary altars.

The next day the pilgrims reached Kan Lu Ssu ("Monastery of Sweet Dew"), the first monastery at the ascent of the holy mountain. Here the pilgrims rested and prepared themselves for their visit to the sanctuary itself.

Kan Lu Ssu is spacious and well adapted as a place of preparation. A mountain stream runs close by and is cleverly diverted into the kitchen and wash-places. Yards with drying facilities, guest-rooms of two storeys and a wide pool provide excellent opportunities for a bath and the washing of clothes. At sunset the pilgrims felt renewed after their wearisome journey on a crowded steamer and their sleepless night in a poor and evil-smelling inn. A day like this of cleansing and preparation at the entry to the sanctuary of Ti-Ts'ang is important in order to secure a good result for one's journey. It is necessary to arrive cleansed in body and soul, clad in clean clothes and with pure and good resolutions. So all took part with great earnestness in the devotions in the temple hall, and as it happened to be a new moon that evening pilgrims and monks gathered together in the temple yard.

Then some of Miao-Chi's fellow-pilgrims came forward with a proposal. They had had, they said, opportunities of hearing

helpful thoughts and discourses from Miao-Chi during the journey. They proposed therefore that he should give an address
upon this day of the new moon. All agreed, and soon Miao-Chi
was standing ready upon the steps. He first mentioned that he
was young and immature and that in many respects he should be
regarded as a seeker. His main topic came spontaneously. With
his keen appreciation of nature, the pure mountain stream had
made an impression upon him. It gave purification and refreshment, a picture of the deepest need of mankind. "We must be
cleansed and purified, a new stream must be led into our lives so
that the grime which covers us and blinds us to the meaning
of life may be washed away. This cleansing stream is repentance
and conversion. Through them alone we come to a clear understanding of our eternal destiny and become aware of the Buddha-
seed that is in every soul. You say that you have no power to
repent and improve yourselves, that you have no knowledge so
as to penetrate into the holy scriptures? But it is just for you who
feel like this that a way has been opened, the way of faith and
self-dedication. In his great mercy Buddha has sent us the great
bodhisattvas. Indeed we can say that he himself has come amongst
us in a new manifestation as merciful King of the Western
Paradise. Dedicate yourselves to him and to his commissioned
bodhisattvas in faith and adoration. No deep learning is required.
You have come to the holy mountain to worship, perhaps not so
much for your own sake as for the sake of a deceased dear one.
Hear then this message; Amitabha, in his great mercy, has sent
Ti-Ts'ang *p'usa* down into the Kingdom of Death in order to
preach the law of salvation. He has the key of the Kingdom of
Death in his hand. He cleanses and refreshes all who seek him."

The next day the company went up to the plateau and there
saw the cluster of monasteries, temples and pagodas spreading out.
The rule is that a pilgrim should make the circuit of all these
sanctuaries, offer a monetary gift at each place and prostrate
himself in front of every altar. It takes at least two days to complete this programme, so poorer folk have two busy days. The
wealthier spend up to a week in order to complete the round.

The most important place is the majestic pagoda which,
according to tradition, has been built over an urn containing the
ashes of Ti-Ts'ang. The pagoda is surrounded by a broad platform,
and here the visitors perform the "sacred ambulation", that is,

they walk with bowed heads and carrying lighted incense-sticks around the base of the pagoda from one hundred to five hundred times, continually reciting formulae of praise to Ti–Ts'ang. It is a common belief that sincerely good people can afterwards, by gazing into a mountain cleft nearby, obtain a vision of the merciful *bodhisattva* at his tireless work of preaching to distressed spirits in the Kingdom of Death. Some dress in a special garb, such as a green robe, and undergo a fast in order to make sure that they will experience this vision.

Among the group of monasteries on the plateau is the age-old Hua Ch'eng Ssu ("Dwindling City Monastery"). Its name found origin in the dominating Buddhist thought that all conceptions of eternity, paradises and heavens are partially true, but are dwindling stages that will ultimately give place to inner, unspeakable reality (Nirvana). Best known is a beautiful pavilion standing at the rear and containing the entire collection of Buddhist scriptures (Tripitaka) given to the monastery by the Emperor Wan-Li of the Ming dynasty.

The next important place is Chi Yuan Ssu with a great pond in front of the entrance. The monastery building is reflected in the water with peculiar clearness and gives the visitor a wonderful impression of grace and calm, and the building's soft lines blend harmoniously with the grandeur of the natural scenery.[1]

Here Miao-Chi and the pilgrims settled down and from it made daily excursions to nearby monasteries. On the moonlit evenings Miao-Chi gathered a constantly-increasing crowd of monks and pilgrims in the temple yard. His fellow-travellers had spoken to others about this remarkable monk who had such ability in preaching the Law of Salvation and who showed such kindness to everyone. The abbot and other leading monks had also become aware of their visitor who so unpretentiously went around giving help and service. Here was a new type, widely different from ordinary worldly-minded "business monks", and different too from high and learned scribes who, in manner and pretensions, sought to lord it over the people. He was soon asked to become a regular teacher in the monastic seminary of Chi Yuan Ssu. Of course he could not bind himself to do this but promised to give a series of lectures to the young men.

So it happened that Miao-Chi stayed about two months in the

---

[1] See an excellent illustration in Prip Møller's *Chinese Buddhist Monasteries*, p. 5.

monastic world of Chiu Hua Shan. Pilgrims, monks and students
gathered around him in gratitude and love. And this love
strengthened and confirmed him in his life vocation as a preacher
and shepherd of souls. No wonder that he always looked back
upon these months as a time of special happiness. He gave
lectures every morning and afternoon mainly on comparative
religion. Besides this he spent much of his time on solitary walks
around the hillside where the Chinese philosopher and statesman,
Wang Yang-Ming, had once spent his best hours.

In the evening he was constantly surrounded by keen young
men. They raised questions and wished to hear as much as possible
of the outer world. Again and again Miao-Chi had to recount his
experiences in Japan and his conversations with Suzuki and Tenko
Nishida, and about the remarkable Francis of Assisi whose
activity had inspired Nishida to begin his social work. It often
ended with a conversation about the great *bodhisattva* of Western
lands, Jesus Christ, who stood behind all these friends of mankind
and gave them spiritual power and enlightenment so that they
were able to accomplish the unbelievable. Miao-Chi already felt
bound with inexplicably strong ties to Christ, and he could
not but repeat his name among the great "world saviours". In this
way many a blessed seed was planted in young minds, and this
Miao-Chi found to be true again and again through later correspondence.

13

Christian Encounter in Hankow

ON A COLD day in January 1921 Miao-Chi stood on the deck of a Yangtse river steamer as it was approaching Hankow. He could see the triple Wuhan cities, so near to one another and yet so different in appearance and in essential characteristics. Hankow and Hanyang are situated on the north bank of the Yangtse but opposite to one another across the swirling waters of the Han tributary which pour into the main river at this point. Wuchang lies on the south bank of the Yangtse and dominates it from the slopes of Serpent Hill with its curious pavilions and temples.

Miao-Chi lodged for a couple of days in a small hotel in Hankow in order that he might feel free to go out and view the place before he bound himself to the scholastic life at Wuchang Academy. He watched with interest the life of the concessions where Westerners, Japanese and wealthy Chinese pursued their business with restless activity. On his way beyond the racecourse he glimpsed the curious low lands behind Hankow, within the shelter of the massive Chang Kung Dyke, where numerous lagoons spread out surrounded by areas of market gardens. On the outskirts of the city, and alongside the railway line, lay a very poor quarter where hundreds and hundreds of squalid huts and tiny wooden shacks propped one another up, surrounded by pools of dirty water. At these pools knelt women washing or rather pounding clothes, while men of all ages carried home big wooden buckets of the same dirty water for cooking rice and preparing tea. It made Miao-Chi shiver. He thought of the clear mountain stream near his home in Formosa and of the springs on Chiu Hua Shan. What a contrast!

Heavy at heart Miao-Chi returned to the town. As he walked

along the street meditating he was suddenly confronted by a fine building with a large tower. The doors stood open and people appeared to be going in and coming out singly or in groups. The fragrance of incense was wafted from the illuminated interior. He concluded that it must be a Christian temple. As he looked cautiously inside the gate a young Chinese, clad in rather an ornate robe, beckoned him in and Miao-Chi suddenly realized that this must be a Roman Catholic place of worship. Some features appeared unfamiliar but there was much that had a homely atmosphere; the candles burning on the altars, the fragrance of incense, the statues of holy men and the radiant Madonna. Around her altar the greater part of the people were assembled, and he gathered that he had arrived during a special mass for her. It was Sunday, the Christians' special day of worship.

He went forward towards the kneeling worshippers who were repeating their *Ave Maria* again and again. Most of them were singing in a foreign tongue while a few held in their hands little Chinese copies of the ritual. Moved by the solemnity, Miao-Chi sank down on his knees by the side of a well-dressed Chinese who let him share his book and indicated to him the Chinese text. It was a hymn of praise to the Holy Mother Mary, the merciful intercessor for all the children of men. Miao-Chi's eyes rested on the features of the statue of Mary; nothing so pure, so winsome or so kind had he ever seen before. Even the most attractive Kuan-Yin images could not compete with this vision. Obviously this must be the Kuan-Yin of the Christians. He sensed that the reality behind these two figures who revealed Divine love must some-how be the same, and with an overflowing heart and liberated mind joined in the praise and prayers. For that reason even the unknown Latin language in which the praise was uttered brought a peculiar warmth of feeling. After a lapse of seven years, when I met him in Formosa, he could quote several phrases of the *Ave Maria*: "*Ave Maria gratia plena, Dominus tecum benedicta tu in mulieribus et benedictus fructus ventris tui Jesu! Sancta Maria Mater Dei ora pro nobis peccatoribus, nunc et in hora mortis nostrae. Amen.*"

The group of worshippers rose and proceeded towards the high altar where three priests in festal robes conducted mass. Over the altar stood a huge image of Christ, the crucified Saviour. Again they knelt down, and Miao-Chi followed suit. He had, of course, read and heard of this great *bodhisattva*, Jesus the Christ, who went so far in his mercy that he allowed himself to be crucified for the sins of the world, but Miao-Chi had never before seen compassion and tragedy so presented as in that huge crucifix. Moved to the bottom of his heart he knelt together with the others. The congregation joined in the responses, and these culminated in a hymn to the "Lamb of God who taketh away the sin of the world":

"*Agnus Dei, qui tollis peccata mundi, Miserere nobis! Dona nobis pacem!*"

After the mass the Chinese who had knelt by the side of Miao-Chi asked him if he would care to see the Roman Catholic institutions alongside the church. This Miao-Chi was more than willing to do. He was led through the orphanage where a crowd of healthy children were playing happily around the courtyard. The friendly guide told him that most of these children had been abandoned in baskets on the streets by poor parents who lived near unhealthy marshes. They proceeded further and came to a department where young men, Westerners and Chinese, lived a monastic life and prepared for the diaconate or to become teachers. Miao-Chi gained a glimpse of them as they returned in solemn procession from service in the church. It was a familiar scene but still different from what he was used to in his own monastery. Finally they came to the hospital. It was overcrowded with patients, invalids and distressed people. There were a few male nurses but the rest of them were nuns clad in a simple brown habit with a black hood over their shoulders. Untiringly they went their rounds attending to the sick.

Miao-Chi came away quite overwhelmed. He walked thoughtfully along Poyang Road wondering if there were more churches and schools that he might see. Two churches came into view upon the right-hand side. One stood by itself, surrounded by a well-kept garden. Some Westerners were entering the door so he thought it must be a special church for foreigners, and it might look incongruous for a Buddhist monk in a grey robe suddenly to appear in that crowd. He chose the other church where many Chinese were gathering. This one was large and appeared to be almost surrounded by school buildings and dormitories. Perhaps it was a mission church. Along came a group of light-hearted students followed by their teachers, and they did not walk in file like the young men at the Roman Catholic church; they chatted and laughed and appeared not at all oppressed by the solemnity. Still, there was an attractive freshness about them; they represented the newer China, a sample of the youths who, through Protestant schools, had found their way into the Christian community.

Miao-Chi had by now penetrated well into the group of buildings. Perturbed, he looked about him; perhaps it would not be wise to venture far in here. He was about to retreat when a friendly voice uttered in the Hankow dialect, "Welcome!" Miao-Chi looked up wonderingly and saw an impressive and kindly-looking Westerner wearing a bishop's cross upon his breast. Soon they were in close conversation. Miao-Chi explained that he was on his way to the Wuchang Academy where he was going to study for two years. He wanted, however, to see something of the "three cities" before he got tied up in academic work and particularly hoped to see the various sanctuaries. The kindly face of the Bishop with his bright smile gave him complete confidence. "Now I propose," said the Bishop, "that we go to evening service in the church here. Later on I will conduct you around our mission station and show you the various sections, but first may I know your honourable name?" "My Buddhist name is Miao-Chi, and I come from Formosa, but I am ashamed that I did not first ask for your honourable name." The Bishop took out his card and Miao-Chi read with wondering eyes the name printed in Chinese and English; "Wu-chu-chiao, Hankow" ("L. H. Roots, Bishop, Hankow Diocese").

The church was nearly full. Young people were in the majority but there were also many over forty, especially of the middle class. Over the altar stood a simple cross, but the image of the suffering Christ was absent from it. Instead, on tablets alongside, were Chinese phrases in classical form, written in large golden characters—"God is great, mighty and holy beyond all words. He is the foundation and pattern of life, and His nature is love. To praise and serve Him is the inmost meaning of life." At the eastern end were beautiful scrolls, and highest of all hung the tablets on which were the Ten Commandments and the Creed.

The service began with a procession of Christian students, led by a cross-bearer, towards the altar. Behind them a Western priest and a Chinese priest walked together, and the Bishop brought up the rear. A short, solemn opening-prayer was offered. On the altar stood two lighted candles flanked by two large vases filled with roses. There was a lectern to bear the Scriptures. Clergy and Bishop then went up into the chancel where stood a row of chairs with kneeling desks. On one side were seated the male members of the choir, on the other side the women, all dressed in blue cassocks with flowing white surplices over them. The main body of the choir consisted of students from the higher classes led by their teachers. Then the notes of the organ pealed out and a flood of harmony resounded through the church.

It was all so overwhelming that Miao-Chi actually felt a shiver running down his spine: but it became still more beautiful when the choir began to sing. Miao-Chi had never imagined that anything so pure and angelic could be produced from human throats. Then came the prayers, and all knelt down. They were not in Latin but in modern Chinese. These prayers were very comprehensive. They embraced not only the needs of the Christian Church but the spiritual and bodily needs of all mankind. The note of praise had been worked finely into the prayers and hymns. One of the deacons proceeded to the lectern which was decorated with a carving of a dove in flight. Miao-Chi sat wondering. In Chinese Buddhism the dove and the white crane are used as symbols of the quiet and powerful activity of the spirit. The deacon read a passage first from the Old Testament and then from the New. Again a hymn was sung and then the sermon began. The preacher was a young Chinese priest who delivered his sermon with warmth and feeling. The main thought was that where the Christian faith gains influence a new and mighty power makes itself felt, not least in practical life. People wake up to realize what they possess in their country and in their culture, and realize afresh their fellowship with the whole of God's world. It sets people free morally and religiously. "China's hope," he said, "must be set in the Christian faith because the best Christian is the best citizen. We Chinese Christians must be as the salt that gives flavour to life and prevents decay and corruption. We all know that our national failing is corruption and with it follows discord. Thus we become as sand grains on a tray and cannot hold together. Without the Christian faith we are afraid to sacrifice ourselves in order to serve others, and that is the reason for the terrible pictures of distress seen in Chinese home life, social life and political life."

It was a kindling address, delivered with tremendous energy and moral conviction. Miao-Chi sat as if petrified. This was something different from the tame though solemn worship in the Roman Catholic church. What he had previously heard must be true, Roman Catholics are the light and Protestants are the salt! Both are needed.

After the service the Bishop took Miao-Chi around and showed him the highly organized school, the bright rooms of the students, the sports ground and the library. Then they went to the Bishop's house and drank tea and talked about the state of Buddhism but they did not again approach the subject of Christianity. It became clear to the Bishop that he had before him a deeply religious and spiritually-minded Buddhist. His remark on leaving was therefore significant: "I have a friend, a Christian missionary, who has taken for special study the religions of the East, particularly Buddhism. He has decided to begin a special mission amongst Buddhists. For the time being he is in Scandinavia in order to awaken interest in this project, but hopes to be back in China next autumn. Will you promise to try to meet him? I believe that it will prove of importance for both of you." Again the Bishop produced one of his cards, this time to write an introduction. Miao-Chi carefully kept the card, and seven years later he presented it to me when the hour finally struck when he and I should meet in Formosa. On the card were these words:

"MY DEAR DR. REICHELT,—I have to-day met this monk of great spiritual development, and feel that it is most desirable that he should come to see you when you return to start your work.

Yours,

LOGAN H. ROOTS"

On the Tuesday following this encounter with Christianity in Hankow Miao-Chi boarded a beamy junk to cross over the Yangtse to Wuchang and the Buddhist Academy. There he took a ricksha to the south side of the city. In front of him in the ricksha were a handbag and a basket, and behind on the hood lay a long bundle of bedding. As he approached the old monastery where the Academy was located a certain apprehension gripped him. The building loomed up out of the flat fields ugly and bare. There was not a tree to be seen, only vegetable gardens and cess-pools and, a little distance away, a small village which seemed to have sprung up in a great hurry because its poorly-constructed huts stood here and there higgledy-piggledy. Evidently it was a place where people from the interior had come seeking work. Miao-Chi overcame his apprehensions; a contented smile lit up his face, for in this neighbourhood there would be ample oppor-tunity for doing social work. Reaching the courtyard he noticed that considerable alterations had been taking place. A two-storied building had been added and in front of the rooms ran a long verandah. From the dormitory a corridor led to the kitchen, baths and lavatories, and then by a back door out to the vegetable gardens and ponds.

The temple hall was impressively flanked by low buildings containing reception rooms, dining rooms and living rooms for some of the temple personnel. Beyond the hall a larger courtyard opened out and around it were constructed new buildings providing two classrooms, a lecture hall and a reading-room. In the upper storey was a large library. Further in, around the third courtyard, were bedrooms for the Rector, teachers and guests. Some decorative plants and shrubs were already growing sturdily. Here within the monastery building the sinister impression involuntarily gained outside quickly disappeared.

Miao-Chi sat down near the door to wait for the host. That is the rule; one must not venture into a monastery until one has met the host and paid one's respects to him. When the host appeared he turned out to be a very tall and stately fellow with a winning face. His home was in Peking where he had been trained under the noted abbot Tao-Kai. His name was Fa-Fang. When ceremonial greetings, with mutual bowing to the floor, had been performed between Miao-Chi and Fa-Fang, the host hastened to the Rector of the Academy, T'ai-Hsü, to announce that the expected student from Formosa had arrived. T'ai-Hsü immed-iately received him. The ceremony of greeting was repeated with this difference, that the Rector made only a slight bow while the student prostrated himself.

A long conversation then followed. It was evident that T'ai-Hsü was pleased to have such a promising student, and one from a distance, in his first seminar.[1] He gave orders that Miao-Chi should be conducted to a single cell, a favour for which the young man was profoundly grateful.

[1] See biographical note on T'ai Hsü, pp. 152-157.

14

Student of Wuchang

THE OPENING SESSION in the lecture hall made a deep
impression upon Miao-Chi. T'ai-Hsü delivered a long address
in which he explained his views and the aims of the academic
activity now about to begin. The main thoughts, according to
Miao-Chi's record, were that the position of Buddhism in China
gave cause for anxiety; superstition, ignorance and corruption
had crept into the order of monks. Hence this, the highest form
of religion, had come into disrepute in the sight of many.
Religion was inseparably linked with the life of man, and was in
fact its foundation, but if religion became contaminated it lost its
power and human life would gradually become empty and
materialistic. In the Christian religion there was a profound saying
of the Founder's. He had said, "Ye are the salt of the earth; ye
are the light of the world!" The Light disperses the darkness of
ignorance so that the way can be seen clearly. Salt not only
prevents decay, it brings flavour, value and grace into life. In
other words, renewal and revolution were needed, not through
external power and force, such as he had tried in the folly of
youth, but by a revolution from within.

Other systems, for instance, Christianity, had their significance
and had been helpful to many but Christianity was inferior in
clear-sightedness and, with its over-emphasis upon the importance of faith and atonement, the highest faculty in man, understanding, did not come into its own.

He then went on to explain the programme of reading and the
curriculum. There would be lectures on the history of Buddhism,
the Buddhist canon, leading ideas of Buddhism, its ethics and the
general history of religion. Considerable time would be spent on
travels and lectures with him, or with his assistant, Professor T'ang.
These travels should be regarded as part of the academic work.

Each week T'ai Hsü would give lectures on the philosophy of the Wei Shih School. He did not conceal his hope that his pupils would concentrate upon the Wei Shih School, for thereby they would "attain to that firmness and that rational and spiritual superiority which ought to mark China's modern interpreters of the sacred writings."

The following day was spent in going through the complex regulations of the Academy. Chinese in general and Buddhists in particular have a great love for detailed regulations. Each branch of activity has minutely worked-out rules and each room has its little notice on the door stating what the room shall be used for. If all these regulations were taken seriously no one could object; rather would it mean complete order and discipline, something very much needed. Unfortunately it is generally implied that when one has finished hanging up all these rules and notices the most important thing has been done and the observance of the regulations is merely of secondary importance.

Miao-Chi soon felt at home in the Academy. It seemed good after a roaming life to settle down in surroundings where he could increase his knowledge and obtain quiet for daily meditation and private studies. The library contained several works on comparative religion. These became his favourite reading and he found a special pleasure in giving his views on religion in essays and monographs. Both T'ai-Hsü and Professor T'ang valued Miao-Chi's written work, and when a new class was opened he was chosen to lecture on comparative religion to the new arrivals. He became very busy but rejoiced in opportunities for work. The climate and diet suited him well, and expeditions with his fellow-students and teachers to various monasteries and temples in the Wuhan cities gave him recreation.

Week-end trips to Hankow were especially interesing. Saturdays and Sundays were used for practical exercises in preaching in the lecture hall and street chapel of the lay Buddhists in Hankow. This was also the regular meeting-place for T'ai-Hsü's thousands of local disciples. The master often gave lectures there and received new disciples. He was serious and impressive as he sat up there on the elevated platform receiving the many genuflections and prostrations from people who had resolved to "take refuge in Buddha, the Doctrine and the Society". After the lectures and solemn acts of initiation they gathered in groups in the smaller rooms. Students acted as hosts and guides, gave short lectures or answered questions in the rooms. In those same rooms children from the street daily received instruction and in the evenings physicians, surgeons and dispensers (all of them disciples of T'ai-Hsü) provided free treatment and medicine for the sick. Crowds were taken up to the roof top in small parties. Here one of the famous *shê-li* stones had been so placed as to be surrounded by a number of mirrors. Electric lights were then switched on, and people could one by one pass the little glass case where the "jewel" was kept, a precious relic found in the ashes of a holy man who had been cremated.

A new and interesting scene was revealed when darkness fell. A door had been opened wide and people from the street poured in to the preaching-chapel where an imposing image of Amitabha stood at the rear. The niche where the image was set up was brilliantly illuminated by electric bulbs. The radiant figure of Amitabha and the music from the organ soon had their effect and the hall became completely filled. A sermon began, followed by short 'testimonies' from the students. T'ai-Hsü had impressed upon his assistants that on such occasions it was best to concentrate upon the message of the Pure Land School, because this was all that ignorant people could understand. In this way Buddhists could compete better with Christians who had made so much progress in China especially through evangelism in street chapels. T'ai-Hsü, who actually had little use for the ways of faith and worship, found it expedient to use this method as a preparation with the crowds.

Miao-Chi and his fellow-students were invited now and then to homes of wealthy Buddhists in Wuchang and Hankow. They were families that had been drawn in by the Revival and naturally welcomed T'ai-Hsü's disciples. These visits brought with them much homeliness and pleasure, but Miao-Chi sensed that they could lead into entanglements, for in those same houses were numerous young men and women who had not undergone any religious experience and were still led by the life of the senses. Miao-Chi felt his youthful blood grow hot in these surroundings. A mirage of sensual attraction threatened the highest and holiest in his life, so there was only one thing to be done and that was to tear himself away from it all and, with greater resolution, devote himself to meditation and work.

F

Extra work lay close at hand, for just outside the Academy lay slum quarters. He had already felt himself called to do something here but during the first happy and busy weeks at the Academy, and again during this period of spiritual weakness amid the favour of men, the impulse had left him. At this awakening he threw himself with renewed ardour into the work. Most people in the slum village had come from the country. Many of them were factory workers, others were ricksha coolies who pulled these light vehicles in Wuchang streets. Continuous shifts with one ricksha are necessary. Some turn out at daybreak because hours are precious. About two o'clock another shift comes on and at night-fall yet another man takes over the job. There is no question of stopping until a morning meal has been prepared; men have to pull on empty stomachs often for hours before a meal can be obtained. Often the profit is so small one day that the whole family is hungry until the afternoon of the next day. Men come back tired and despondent and often their wives and children return home worn and exhausted from the city and its surround-ings where they have perhaps gathered a little fuel or begged for money. Sometimes they are fortunate enough to get a decent meal, but more often it is insufficient and if they have some money to spare it is often thrown away on gambling and opium smoking. People such as these inhabited the miserable huts near the Academy. The crowded village held about five hundred people but there was no school for children and no one to look after the sick and suffering.

Among his fellow-students Miao-Chi had found a friend who in many respects shared his ideals of life. He came from Szechuan and was named Hua-Lin ("Flowery Forest"). He was an able student and a tender-hearted fellow who was very willing to help the destitute. Miao-Chi and Hua-Lin formulated their plan to open a school for the children and a welfare association for the sick, the destitute and unemployed. It was first necessary to obtain permission, so together they went to see T'ai-Hsü and put forward their project. To their great joy they met with complete sympathy, and indeed T'ai-Hsü became enthusiastic about the plan. He wrote a letter of recommendation which the two friends could show to the philanthropic members of the Buddhist Laymen's Society in Wuchang, and it was not long before they had collected the necessary funds. A teacher was appointed and the two friends assisted in the instruction whenever they had spare time. They also used to go around to the sick with medicines, dressing wounds and distributing articles to the needy. Soon they were known in every hut. A smile came over hardened and embittered faces whenever the two monks appeared in their grey gowns. Children ran out happily to meet them and fathers and mothers welcomed them at the doors.

Sometimes Miao-Chi and Hua-Lin gathered the adults in an open place for popular lectures and discussions. Subjects varied from demands of hygiene to the highest needs of man, deliverance and salvation from the chains of sin and the slavery of ignorance. A new spirit came over the gloomy village; cheerfulness and gratitude became general. Only a gang over in the local opium den cast looks of hatred in the direction of the two "disturbers of the peace".

In yet another field of work Miao-Chi was able to make a notable contribution. T'ai-Hsü had noticed that Christian missionaries and some Chinese evangelists had obtained permission from the authorities to visit the public gaols in order to speak to the prisoners. It was even described in the newspapers because quite a number of prisoners had become converted and had left the gaols as new men. This challenged T'ai-Hsü. Why should not Buddhists do the same? He placed the matter before his students, and of course everybody offered for service. T'ai-Hsü applied to the authorities and permission was given.

For some months it went with a swing. Prisoners used to gather in a large room and young Buddhist monks in their dignified robes performed with the greatest eloquence as "teaching masters" to this mixed audience. They too were "written up" in the newspapers. But it was not long before it became too commonplace a thing; more and more of the preachers fell away and finally the whole scheme broke down. T'ai-Hsü was disappointed, and on one occasion mentioned it to Miao-Chi and Hua-Lin. They declared themselves willing to continue, not only with lectures for the prisoners, but they wished to visit them in their cells in order to do personal work. They were faithful; throughout the two years that still remained of their college course Miao-Chi and Hua-Lin regularly visited the public prisons in order to awaken and help the unfortunate.

15

Summer Vacation on Nan Yoh

THAT FIRST SUMMER vacation at Wuchang Academy became a lengthy one because T'ai-Hsü and Professor T'ang had received invitations to visit certain monasteries and lay societies in Central China. T'ai-Hsü chose some of his most promising students to go with him, among them Miao-Chi. They were to make a record of his lectures and assist as preachers, give interviews and organize study circles and local associations. Besides this they were to have a summer course with their master in a country location in Hunan.

After a varied and interesting lecture tour in the cities of Changsha and Siangtan T'ai-Hsü proceeded with his group of students southwards across the Siang River in order to reach Nan Yoh Shan ("Southern Peak Mountain"). Here it was intended that he and the students should have their summer course and some weeks of rest and recreation.

They travelled aboard one of the small steamers which, during the high water season (summer), go up river as far as Hengyang. The morning was brilliant and the scenery of Hunan expanded in all its beauty before the eyes of the travellers. It was not long before they saw the dominating background of Nan Yoh Shan. Like a strong protecting arm the lofty mountain peak, with its many ridges, rose upon the horizon only a few miles away.

Just before sunset they arrived at a large and stately Buddhist monastery, Chu Sheng Ssu ("Monastery of the Holy Blessing"), situated near the entrance to the little temple-town of Nan Yoh. A graceful flight of steps leads up to the monastery with the bamboo grove as its background. Everything is in the grand classical style, showing the favour and esteem bestowed upon the monastery by emperors and powerful men throughout the centuries. This monastery now became the base for T'ai-Hsü and his group of young men, for there was everything they needed; a large temple and lecture halls, well-equipped monastic cells and easy access to the mountains and hills with their numerous monasteries.

It was evident that T'ai Hsü and his students would thrive well in these magnificent surroundings. The lectures were well attended by monks from surrounding temples and monasteries and by quite a number of laymen and pilgrims also. The Monastery of the Holy Blessing had again become the centre of Nan Yoh Shan's religious world. It was a picturesque sight to see groups of monks in their flowing robes solemnly proceeding down the hillsides and through the temple town. Many had come a long way for the lectures, and a light meal, consisting of rice and mixed vegetables, was served to them. This latter dish, called *lo-han-ts'ai* ("dish of the holy men") is nourishing and appetizing; cabbage, carrots, soya beans, rice and bean oil are the main ingredients.

Miao-Chi was happy during his summer visit; attendances at the lectures were good and the place afforded a rare opportunity of studying the classic organization of worship in ancient China. He studied in particular the impressive temple in the town of Nan Yoh. This immense temple is totally unlike ordinary Buddhist and Taoist temples and is called "Sheng Ti Ta Miao" ("Great Temple of the Holy God"). It was built somewhat in the style of those enormous temples of literature (*wen miao*) that used to be found in China's large cities in honour of Confucius and his school. It was restored and modernized by a rich and highly-respected scholar, Wang Lan-Hsiang, some years ago but its history goes back about two thousand five hundred years. A fine avenue of willow trees leads up to the main building graced with a colossal tower and three gates. Here it was that imperial edicts used to be read. Inside one comes to the Red Pavilion where there is a monumental tablet upon which the Emperor K'ang-Hsi wrote the dedication in an excellent flowery style. The tablet is borne upon the back of an immense tortoise[1] carved in stone. The figure has been worn smooth by many hands throughout the centuries because in this way innumerable pilgrims reckoned to obtain personal contact with the "Holy Ruler" of the mountain.

In ancient times there was a special priesthood connected with

---

[1] The tortoise used to be the symbol of eternity.

this central sanctuary on Nan Yoh. Afterwards the administration came into Taoist hands but when the Buddhists rose to power they naturally had to be included, and now for centuries Buddhists and Taoists have divided the sanctuary between them. The former have the left-hand side of the building, and this part is called the Six Temples with the Common Gate and is attended by fifteen monks. On the right-hand side the Taoists have their department, which is called the Monastery of the Three Basic Elements. Here the rules are not so strict, so that many pilgrims who find it difficult to abstain from animal food prefer to lodge here. Miao-Chi spent much of his spare time in studying this temple; it seemed like a voice from ancient times. Both here and at the Monastery of the Holy Blessing he found in the archives many interesting documents that threw light upon the history of religion in China.

Later in the summer it was decided that T'ai-Hsü and his students should spend a couple of weeks in visiting the other large Buddhist monasteries situated on the eastern slopes of Nan Yoh Shan. The young men went first and the leaders were taken in carrying-chairs. It is quite an undertaking to attempt the trip in one day, because the mountain is about five thousand feet high and the road is very difficult. Speed was unnecessary for T'ai-Hsü's pilgrims; they were to give lectures in monasteries and stay for two or three days in each place.

The highest monastery, Shan Feng Ssu ("Monastery of the Mountain Summit"), is actually situated some distance from the peak but is approximately thirteen miles from the foot of the mountain. Wind and weather wreak havoc up there so windows and doors must be strong and solid and the whole construction is of heavy granite blocks and unusually thick brick. A wonderful spring gushes out close by the road and gives water to the monastery and to a smaller Taoist temple in the neighbourhood.

Of still greater interest is a temple built into the summit itself and called Chü Ran Feng ("Lord of Fire Peak"). The name is significant for here the genius of the mountain often reveals itself in majesty—with lightning, thunder, fierce storms, gloomy clouds and torrential rain. It is a place of awe, the Sinai of Hunan, because the "Holy Ruler" (Sheng Ti) reveals himself here as the fire god. Even on a relatively quiet and peaceful day pilgrims are overshadowed by awe, for the place is the most holy and majestic on Nan Yoh Shan. One is supposed to talk only in whispers and a meal must be partaken of in silence.

The temple is built of granite and the roof covered with iron plates. Pilgrims as a rule reach the mountain top in the afternoon, tired and dripping with sweat. A cup of warm tea and a towel dipped in warm water provide welcome refreshment before they start upon an important act of worship. In a side room, cut out of the mountain, sits a monk selling candles, bundles of incense-sticks and imitation money. The room is barely large enough for a bed, a desk and a shelf to hold the goods for sale.

In the entrance hall are placed large incense urns, for it is not sufficient to light one, two, or three incense-sticks; large bundles are expected. No wonder that the urns during the pilgrim season used to glow red-hot for the greater part of the day and a cloud of smoke obscured the roof beams. This is the case too in the inner hall where the "Holy Ruler" sits enthroned over the altar, severe and commanding. His statue stands in a large glass case, fortified with a thick wooden lattice-work so that it may not be irreparably spoilt by the smoke. Pilgrims kneel down in front of the statue and there is heard the formula of adoration, "Reverently I offer homage to thee, O divine majesty, and implore thee to have mercy!"

After the worship pilgrims return to the entrance hall where steaming rice, with bowls of *lo-han-ts'ai*, stand waiting. With growing interest Miao-Chi observed these various scenes, and he felt as though his heart would burst with emotion, so moved was he by the religious atmosphere. Nevertheless he felt a deep pain in his heart as he saw clearly that all this worship was terribly confused and permeated with the most dreadful superstition. Sitting with the pilgrims out in the entrance hall he observed that its walls were covered with small wooden tablets. On these had been written various texts of gratitude. These had been sent by grateful pilgrims from country districts and towns in Hunan who believed that they had been favoured in their prayers after the exacting pilgrimage. One sentence constantly recurred, and it is seen hung up in nearly every Buddhist temple: *yu-ch'iu-pi-ying* ("he who prays, obtains"). What chiefly impressed Miao-Chi was the sight of a large wooden tablet on which was carved a single golden character: *hsin* ("heart"), the unknown donor wishing, in this discreet but significant way, to remind pilgrims of the fact that what is important is the hidden life of the heart.

And now company after company of pilgrims descend the mountain side, for they must reach one of the monasteries before nightfall. Pilgrim hymns sound more and more remote and finally even the noise of firecrackers dies away in the cool evening breeze. Once again the summit of Nan Yoh Shan is deserted except for six or seven Buddhist priests who walk quietly about among the smoking urns. There is a good-humoured smile upon their faces, seeing that the day has brought large sums into the temple chest.

16

Second Year at Wuchang

THE NEW SESSION at Wuchang was different and the reason obvious. Most of the new students were immature and some of them bore marks of an indulgent life. A few months after the brilliant opening ceremonies had taken place the difficulties and complications began to make themselves felt. For Miao-Chi and the senior students it became difficult because they had to help to a certain extent as assistant teachers. Among the newcomers was a small group that entered sincerely and zealously into their studies, but the majority consisted of youths who held that they had made so much progress that they stood in no need of any guidance, still less any correction, from senior students. There was another difficulty; at that time patriotic feeling ran high, and many students of the Academy maintained that it was their right and duty to follow the spirit of the times. In the reading-room were laid out a number of modern periodicals and these contained things both good and evil. Several magazines were not only decidedly atheistic but also anti-religious.

T'ai-Hsü of course had no objection to an atheistic tendency. It was part of his programme to show how foolish it is to base one's outlook on life upon the idea of a personal god. He soon realized, however, that these periodicals were a two-edged sword, for even Buddhism was being attacked as antiquated superstition. So the periodicals were removed and the same fate befell several political pamphlets which, in spite of containing many good and sound ideas about reform, propagated in a cunning way a loose morality and the radical dissolution of society. It soon appeared moreover that the trouble could not be stopped merely by prohibiting these periodicals. Contagion was in the air and groups of students elsewhere, who regarded themselves as leaders in patriotism, had their own ways of keeping young men at the Buddhist Academy informed in regard to new tendencies. It became an easy matter for agitators from outside to form cells within the Academy. Results followed inevitably—participation in secret meetings in the city, other tasks of a kind and scope clearly irreconcilable with the nature of religion, accompanied by a waning interest in the curriculum of the Academy and a reduced interest in meditation and other religious exercises.

The leader of the bad elements was an able, eloquent and aggressive monk from one of the Wuhan cities. He had chosen the name of Ku-Yin ("Note of Pain"). This was to signify his deep compassion and, at the same time, his pessimistic outlook. Greater irony has never been put into a name because Ku-Yin was a decided example of arrogance and heartlessness. Before becoming a monk he had made connections with the underworld and as a monk he had debased himself by acquiring some of the vices of the Buddhist dregs.

Ku-Yin soon became the "best friend" of agitators outside. Secretly he and his cronies bribed the watchmen so that they could sneak out and in during the night to take part in political meetings that were held in Wuchang. After the meetings they visited brothels and gambling-dens. With anxiety the teachers noticed increasing listlessness among the students, and when they later found that libellous placards had been pasted on walls outside the main gate and in the neighbourhood it became clear that a conspiracy had been organized. On these placards Fa-Fang, Miao-Chi and Hua-Lin were accused in a most repulsive way. This slanderous practice is common in a monastery when it is desired to harm leaders but during normal times no one takes much notice.

T'ai-Hsü and his assistants knew of these matters and had occasionally been the object of attacks, but seen in connection with the whole situation the leaders felt that they ought to get to the bottom of the matter. It was decided to have a parade and roll-call at an unexpected time and an investigation of the students' correspondence was undertaken. The parade took place at night. It then appeared that Ku Yin and nine of his clique were absent. In their rooms were found a number of compromising writings, obscene pictures and dangerous documents that revealed revolutionary connections. Next day a trial was held and even

Ku-Yin's eloquence could not save him. All were expelled. During the following weeks a number of other students who had had close connection with Ku-Yin disappeared. They felt the ground hot beneath them and quietly withdrew under the pretext of sickness at home, and so on. In this way the student group was reduced to thirty.

Miao-Chi and other senior students knew that the danger was not yet over; Ku-Yin and his gang would know how to exact revenge. The troublemaker himself was too cowardly to take part in an attack, and he sought hired assistants. He understood where to find such people, namely in the secret organization of expelled monks existing in all Chinese cities. As a rule these men have no temple in which to stay but simply drift as vagabonds and are significantly called *yeh-ho-shang* ("wild monks"). They live by begging, robbery and intimidation. In return for a sum of money Ku-Yin was promised full assistance by a notorious gang of wild monks. At last in early summer there seemed an opportunity for Ku-Yin to achieve his object. An accomplice in the Academy revealed that at such and such a time after nightfall several of the senior students would be returning from a meeting at a neighbouring monastery. On a narrow path Miao-Chi and his comrades were suddenly surrounded by a body of these wild men armed with knives and sticks. Miao-Chi was felled to the ground and a knife struck him in the chest; the others escaped with blows. It was found that the knife had glanced off a bone, so the lung was unharmed, but Miao-Chi bled heavily and had to stay in bed for a considerable time.

Miao-Chi was grateful for a second summer vacation because the heavy loss of blood had reduced his powers and the nervous shock he had sustained had not yet been completely overcome. By the help of influential friends T'ai-Hsü had secured one of the temples at Kuling which remained after the Taiping Rebellion, a friendly little place called Ta Lin Ssu ("Temple of the Great Forest"). In this way T'ai-Hsü gradually realized his plan of large annual conferences for Buddhists. When Miao-Chi visited Kuling it was quite lively at Ta Lin Monastery, and he and his fellow-students had frequent opportunities for meeting interesting men of religion from other places and groups.

The greatest thrill, however, was the opportunity for long mountain walks that continually offered new and impressive views across the plains, the Poyang Lake and long stretches of distant mountains in the west. At times entire groups of students, as well as Buddhist scholars from Wuhan and Shanghai, went out on the mountains together. Miao-Chi often went out on solitary walks and these were most rewarding. Sometimes he visited the mountain-tops but more often would choose a valley where some racing stream, a little temple and numerous ruins told their tale of religious life of old. Here stood majestic cedars, and from their tops he heard again the peculiar rushing sound that had once impressed him during his stay on Koyasan.

During his walks at Kuling Miao-Chi often met Westerners who had come up to Kuling during the hottest months. On Sunday mornings the windows of Union Church were generally open, and the singing rang out melodiously in the clear mountain air. And how they could sing, those foreigners! Miao-Chi went as close as he dared and often felt a strong desire to enter and sit near the door, but there was his monk's robe to be considered. However, the problem was soon solved; one of his friends had with him a long raincoat and Miao-Chi borrowed it one Sunday and found a corner in the church. His English was not good enough for him to follow everything. Still, he experienced a profound impression at the service. The prayers, hymns and Scripture reading, as well as the atmosphere of devotion, affected him deeply.

During the spring term of 1923 the waves of revolution again began to run high. China's youth was disappointed over the constant failure of the country to achieve a truly democratic form of government. The Central Government was weak while the peasants were oppressed and harried by robber bands. Hence there was ample material to be set alight by inflammatory propaganda. Wuchang government authorities soon became aware that it was in educational establishments that their real critics and opponents were to be found. They had spies everywhere, and every now and then they struck at one school or another, imprisoned teachers and students, and, by means of fearsome tortures, obtained compromising documents and names of sympathizers. Nor was it long before Wuchang Academy was surrounded and thoroughly searched. The students concerned were, of course, imprisoned, and it was only the influence of T'ai-Hsü and some prominent lay Buddhists in higher official circles that saved them from execution. As might be expected the majority of students did not dare remain in Wuchang, and only T'ai-Hsü's loyal nucleus and a few junior students remained. It was almost time for Miao-Chi to think about his departure too. With other leading students he received his diploma as a graduate of Wuchang Academy.

After a moving farewell from teachers and fellow-students he crossed the temple courtyard towards the village. Here the school-children stood at attention on both sides of the road and behind them a row of mothers with babies in their arms. The children sang one of the songs which Miao-Chi had taught them and the mothers waved to him while tears rolled down their cheeks. Teachers and fellow-students watched from a distance. Professor T'ang expressed their feeling in the words: "To-day a true *bodhi-sattva* has left our academy. May fortune and blessing follow him!"

17

Buddhism Salutes a Master

THERE WAS NO little excitement amongst lay Buddhists in Shanghai at Miao-Chi's arrival amongst them. It was their first opportunity to hear one of T'ai-Hsü's newly-fledged masters and their hall was filled. Excitement increased when, after opening devotions, Miao-Chi ascended the platform and took the seat of a *fa-shih*. His method was different from that of traditional masters. They always take a certain Buddhist text as the basis for a lecture. Miao-Chi announced that he would speak of the nature and forms of expression of religious life as seen in the light of Buddhism and other great religions. In other words, it would be viewed from the standpoints of psychology of religion and comparative religion. In a clearly-constructed lecture, delivered with a warmth of genuine feeling and concern for mankind, he spoke boldly upon the central thoughts of religion with constant references to the basic sayings of leading Buddhist, Taoist and Hindu authors. With this he linked a short exposition of the main Christian ideas, after which he issued a personal challenge to adopt the religious life, not as an experiment in thought but as the true life of the heart. Religion, he argued, would then become important to the individual as well as to the collective life of mankind.

Day after day for a whole week he adhered to this line of thought and day by day the audience increased so that finally they had to move into a larger hall. It was significant too that more and more students and upper class people attended. This was something new, and many were perturbed. Was this Buddhist teaching? Was this orthodox doctrine? Some venerable *fa-shih* and older lay monks shook their heads with misgiving; it smacked of modernism, but the majority of the audience were enraptured.

The lectures were repeated in another part of the city, namely Chapei, and Dr. Ting Fu-Pao arranged that Miao-Chi should be invited to lecture in two of the larger monasteries in the city. Of still greater significance was the work that Miao-Chi accomplished among small groups that daily gathered around him for conversation and guidance. It was here too that he began to feel inadequacy and limitation because he had a far wider horizon than other *fa-shih*. Moreover he had had some sacred experience of the importance of "breaking through" and knew the significance of faith and meditation, and he constantly experienced the wonder of having been brought into the mystical life of the universe. Nevertheless he felt that something essential was missing, and many a time when he saw questioning and imploring eyes directed towards him he felt an impulse to hide his face and flee away. He felt that he had not yet solved the most important question about the idea of God as central in the life of man, and that he did not, therefore, have sufficient spiritual capital for the demands of this work of shepherding souls. If this problem could be solved he felt that his calling, his longings and abilities lay along these lines.

After a month of intensive work in Shanghai, Miao-Chi travelled to Hangchow, that gracious and historical city situated on the shores of the West Lake. It is one regarded with special favour by all Chinese, and many nourish a secret longing to visit the place at least once. Together with neighbouring Soochow, Hangchow possesses a network of canals, picturesque bridges and lotus lakes dotted over with curious islands and pavilions and surrounded by beautiful temples and monasteries. All this fascinating loveliness is summed up in the proverb, "Above is heaven; below are Soochow and Hangchow". There is something that Soochow does not possess and that is Hangchow's captivating background of hill slopes and mountain valleys. Here and along the lakes are found Hangchow's famous temples, monasteries, pagodas, ancestral halls and mausoleums. Vegetation is rich and the songs of birds in the tree tops are strikingly attractive and melodious. No wonder that Buddhist scholars in their compositions often refer to the West Lake as a symbol of the Western Paradise, the Pure Land of the All-Father, Amitabha, where the redeemed gather after death.

After his exacting time in Shanghai, Miao-Chi's stay in Hangchow became a welcome time of recreation. True, he had to give a number of lectures in laymen's societies and in the larger monasteries, but there were days of rest in between, and several wealthy lay Buddhists were unremitting in asking him to take part in long tours in the neighbourhood or in social gatherings at vegetarian restaurants. These gatherings brought him into relationship with numbers of religious people who had already become animated through his lectures. Some of them had actually been "converted" and fervent anticipation shone in their eyes when they met Miao-Chi in private interviews to talk about life's problems.

His first visit in the monastic world of Hangchow was to the ancient Ling Yin Ssu ("Monastery Under the Spirits' Shadow"), lying secluded in a picturesque mountain valley, surrounded by rocks, caves and bamboo groves. T'ai-Hsü's personal friend, who had taken the Taoist name of Yu-Huang, was abbot at that time. It was evidently a great favour for this prelate to take Miao-Chi around personally to show him the monastery buildings, for there are few who are allowed to see "His Highness". At that time an almost unmanageable crowd of visitors used to come to see the place day after day; streams of cars and rickshas stopped in front of the gatehouse and every day several hundreds of pilgrims travelled on foot in order to come under the secret shadow and blessing of the spirits. For all that the immense temple courtyard rarely gave the impression of being overcrowded.

The temple hall itself, recently restored, is magnificent. Colossal beams from Oregon have been adorned with fine painting and ornamentation, and the three Buddha figures are rich with mosaic work. The sparkling jewels between the eyebrows and on the blue headgear are unique in luminosity and depth of colour.

From the Ling Yin Monastery Miao-Chi proceeded further up the valley to Hu Pao Ssu ("Tiger Leopard Monastery"). The place is best known as the favourite spot of the famous governor, Su Tung-Po. Here he sat and wrote some of his renowned poems whenever he was able to tear himself away from his official duties. It is said that he could be found working at any time of the day or night, for his aim was to render the changing colour-play of the mountains, hills and lakes in his singular word paintings.

Miao-Chi also visited Yü Ch'uan Ssu ("Jade Fountain Monastery"), standing under a pine and bamboo-covered hill and, with its bubbling spring and pools, offering visitors a shady retreat during summer heat. The monks at Yü Ch'uan Ssu prepare special cakes which are bought by visitors who wish to feed the fish. These fish are bought by pious people who in this way accumulate "merit" for themselves by setting them free. Here within the temple pond the fish are never caught for food; they live until they die of old age, and then they will, according to Buddhist thought, enter upon a new and better existence. The same destiny is expected for various domestic animals that are bought and given to Buddhist temples. Many of the fish at Yü Ch'uan Ssu are very old because of the excellent nourishment provided. Still more long-lived are a number of tortoises that crowd together on the steps leading down to the pools. The marks on their shells reveal that they may be hundreds of years old.

There was no lack of pressing invitations from leading Buddhists to have Miao-Chi as a youth worker and *fa-shih* in Shanghai, Hangchow or even the neighbouring town of Ningpo. Miao-Chi nevertheless felt that it was his duty to return to his sponsors in Formosa, and he looked forward to being able to work for the good of Formosa itself. He secured a passage southwards on a coaster and stopped off at Amoy.

Here Miao-Chi went out into the country, an hour's journey on foot over the hills, to a monastery of modern foundation, Nan P'u T'o ("Southern P'u T'o"), where a celebrated *fa-shih*, Chang-Hsin, had accomplished good ground work for the opening of a Buddhist academy in South China. A number of T'ai-Hsü's prominent graduates from Wuchang were on the staff, and T'ai-Hsü would very much have liked Miao-Chi to become a permanent teacher there. That Miao-Chi came to visit the academy at this time seemed providential because it had recently passed through one of its student crises during which serious disturbances had occurred. The result was that fifteen students were expelled.

The wounds were still unhealed when Miao-Chi reached Amoy, but the new spirit that he brought greatly helped to restore harmony. His first lecture worked wonders. His subject was the task of young Buddhists. The students had often heard T'ai-Hsü and other teachers treat this topical subject, but here was a difference. In the first place Miao-Chi included himself, using the "we" form; he himself belonged to the new generation that would give

Buddhism its true place in communal life. Here is a short extract
from Miao-Chi's diary describing one of his lectures:

> In order to help people to an understanding of the inner consciousness of
> life it is insufficient to know the catchwords and thoughts of New Buddhists.
> One must lead the religious life in earnest and have one's joy, goal and ideal
> there. Only thus can one become a living witness. The elders spoke of
> "having broken through" and some of us have been fortunate enough to
> meet people who have actually broken through. I met some of these people
> in Japan and have met some of them here in China. Most of them have
> broken through by earnest and methodical meditation, and some through
> sincere and persistent prayer. I mention something else that has been of help
> to me: the study of comparative religion and especially of religious geniuses
> who have opened up new visions to the religious world. A Buddhist of the
> new sort must then, in my opinion, become a true *"ho-shang"* (Buddhist
> monk in China). You know what is implied in this beautiful name, which
> has now, I am sorry to say, been dragged down into the mud; *"ho"* means
> harmonious and *"shang"* is exalted, thus meaning a man who lives in an
> exalted state of harmony and who helps people to lead a harmonious life.
>
> I do not imply that one must become an ordained monk in order to enter
> upon this highest form of life. The greatest man whom I have met upon this
> earth was a layman. He had received much help through his Buddhist studies
> but the decisive "break-through" came when he began to study Christianity.
> I am thinking of Tenko Nishida in Japan, the man who now does so much as
> a social reformer and religious leader. This man radiates a wonderful peace,
> serenity and love. Nishida told me how reading the biography of a disciple
> of Christ brought him suddenly to see the "inner light". With this light
> followed power and joy. I got hold of this book later on and it shed light
> upon my path. The book is about the saintly Francis of Assisi, a follower of
> the great master Jesus who became poor in order to make us rich. The secret
> is to serve one's fellow men while recognizing that we are all partakers of
> one communal life. By leading this life we are led out of isolation and enter
> into liberation. Think what it would mean if our Buddhist academies could
> produce a generation of youth that has discovered this wonderful secret
> of life!

It seemed as though a new breath of life had come into the
group of young men who listened to those words. No wonder
that they asked to be present at the public lectures delivered by
Miao-Chi in the city. Some followed him when he travelled to
neighbouring towns. His stay had to be prolonged until mid-
summer but at the end of July Miao-Chi tore himself away and
boarded a little steamer which (in normal times) plies between
Amoy and Takow, the southern port of Formosa. The Formosa
Channel is sometimes difficult to cross when there is a strong
current and a high wind. Miao-Chi was fortunate in having a

quiet day for his crossing. At sunset the ship reached a position where the majestic ranges of Formosa began to show up above the horizon. It was more than five years since he had seen the island. What experiences, rich and painful, those years had brought! Now at last he would be able to begin his work in earnest.

ABBOT AND DISCIPLE

18

Family Festival

EARLY THE NEXT day, July 30, 1923, Miao-Chi took train from the port of Takow, in south-west Formosa, and by late afternoon had arrived many miles inland at the tiny railway station of Piao Miao, from where the light railway goes in towards Ta Hu Valley. It was too late to think of travelling further that night so he stayed at an inn. At daybreak Miao-Chi boarded a trolley and a few hours later had reached his home district. There lay Ta Hu ("Great Lake"), deep blue as ever. Mountain streams rushed down turbulently, well-wooded hills stood clothed in summer garb and the paddy fields, just planted for the second time, were showing that light green colour which renders even the most prosaic fields in East Asia attractive and fresh. Everything was so familiar and yet everything appeared to have shrunk dreadfully now that he had seen so much of the world outside.

Miao-Chi had written home notifying his family so they were not surprised that morning to see him walking up towards the house. He was somewhat bent and his face showed that he had gone through trouble, but the light in his eyes was stronger and something peaceful seemed to be expressed in his features.

They hurried out to meet him. The eldest brother, Lo Chi-Ying, who was a teacher, stood there with wife and children. Lo Fu-Ying, who managed the farm, had married a Hakka woman and already had two little children at his side. In front of the group stood the old father in a monk's robe. Miao-Chi had heard by letter of his father having taken this step. In a way he was glad, but not entirely, for he was already doubtful whether Buddhism was the complete solution. Miao-Chi prostrated himself before his father in accordance with old Chinese etiquette. As a Buddhist he repeated the prostration twice again. The brothers he greeted by bowing slightly with his hands together.

Towards his sisters-in-law he made a half turn, but the children were too much for him; before he was aware of it he had them all around him and the youngest he took into his arms.

Soon his bags were opened and from them he drew out parcels wrapped in red paper and labelled with neatly-written Chinese characters. No one had been forgotten. There were works of art for his father and brothers; gold hairpins, ornaments and rolls of cloth for the sisters-in-law; fountain-pens and electric torches for the older boys, and tops and sweets for the smaller children.

In the meantime breakfast had been prepared, and over steaming bowls a lively conversation flowed without restraint, and the family, now re-united after five years of separation, was able to experience a festive atmosphere again. Naturally Miao-Chi was asked to lead evening devotions.

The next day he paid a visit to the familiar monastery on the mountain, and here he was received as a guest of honour by the Abbot and leading monks. The Abbot decided that Miao-Chi should be given a short rest before entering upon full service at the monastery, and therefore proposed that he should stay at home for a while. Miao-Chi rejoiced that in this way he could be of help to his family.

The seventh anniversary of their mother's death occurred at this time, and all felt that the day should be observed. The eldest brother, Lo Chi-Ying, as a recognized scholar, was given the task of writing the long scrolls to be hung up alongside the house altar. Miao-Chi composed a poem to be read at the grave during the memorial service and which would be sent over to "the other side" through purifying flames of fire. Memorial writings are often composed in rhythmic style, the biographical data being followed by lofty reflections in classical language coined from the works of Confucianism, Buddhism and Taoism. Here is experienced the truth of the oft-quoted saying, "the three religions are one", and the well-known proverb about the lotus—"red petals, white roots and green leaves belong to one and the same plant". In China most religious people think and live according to this viewpoint; they do not belong to any single religion but find their religious values in a synthesis of Buddhism, Taoism and Confucianism. This was true of the Lo family. As for Miao-Chi, there was in addition an extensive study of Hinduism and in his later years some study of Christianity as well.

The day before the memorial service brought brilliant weather following one of Formosa's violent "summer baths" with peals of thunder and teeming rain. Streams brawled and chattered down their courses, raindrops lay glittering like pearls on every leaf and a wonderful freshness of life appeared to emanate from field and forest. The burial ground of the Lo family lay some distance in the hills, so it became a hot climb for young and old. They walked in white mourning garments and with burning incense-sticks in their hands. As the procession passed the houses of neighbours loud salvoes of crackers were discharged.

In front went a small band with flutes, gongs and drums. They discharged their duties with the utmost vigour, for if there is anything the Chinese dislike on such occasions it is heavy silence and depressing solemnity. All this goes strongly against our Western temperament and feeling, and many Westerners pronounce harsh judgments upon these noisy festivals. That criticism is understandable, not least when one takes into account the hired carriers of banners and emblems, all of them shabbily dressed, for whom the entire proceedings are like a fair.

There is, however, generally an inner circle of friends and relations present who, in deep sorrow and with deeply-moved minds, follow everything. For them grave stillness and gloomy solemnity would be unseemly, not to say offending to the deceased and the bereaved. But sorrow too must find expression, and it must be demonstrated that the deceased is bitterly missed. For showing this feeling the nearest female relations are responsible, and if there are only a few of them a group of "weeping women" is engaged, and this act tends to be just as much overdone in its intensity as lively flute and gong noises or the deafening salvoes of fireworks.

The mourning festival of the Lo family proceeded in restrained fashion. Both Chi-Ying and Miao-Chi did everything possible to introduce dignity into the proceedings. Following the band walked the eldest brother, who carried a framed portrait of the deceased. After him followed the father, supported by his two younger sons, and then came uncles, cousins and other relatives and the group of nine children, all wearing white garments bound around the waist with girdles of rice straw, and white caps and white shoes. At the grave there was more music and more setting off of crackers. The portrait was set up on the grave and lighted candles were placed between smoking incense-sticks. Then the sons came forward and made their obeisances, after which Miao-Chi, as a priest, conducted the Buddhist memorial mass. His well-trained voice, the sincerity with which the mass was conducted, but even more the beautiful tablet and the memorial writing which he read aloud moved his audience. The written scroll was then solemnly brought to the candles and slowly consumed. In the meantime all knelt for several minutes, and several persons present were moved to silent tears. It was a memorable occasion.

19

A Buddhist Reformation

A DAY OR TWO after the memorial service Miao-Chi and his father settled in at Fa Yün Ssu. His father had stayed there a couple of years already and found himself entirely at home in that quiet monastic world on the mountain. As an old and recognized scholar he enjoyed much freedom of movement and daily visited various points of vantage where, with his deep sense of nature's beauty, he could give himself up to poetry and meditation. It was only when important documents had to be prepared for the authorities that his assistance was required. Otherwise he was relieved of routine work and could cultivate his own interests. He was always to be found at devotions, even at night mass, and he displayed a deep and genuine interest in all spiritual exercises. He thus became one of the many officials in East Asia who used to devote themselves to religious studies towards the close of life.

In the case of Miao-Chi some excitement was noticeable amongst the Abbot and leading monks. When young and able monks had previously been granted permission to visit foreign lands the results had been widely different. Some had returned with all the manners of perfected masters but with little spiritual character. Here was someone who had graduated from T'ai-Hsü's famous academy and had already won a name as teacher and lecturer. No wonder that the first month especially was exciting for the leaders of this chief monastery of Formosa. Miao-Chi himself was for a long time unaware of this air of questioning. His mind was filled with gratitude and happiness at arriving home after rich and exacting years abroad. The important thing now was to work and serve, to make a positive contribution and harness all his constructive powers.

The Abbot and other leading monks soon began to find that it

was a new Miao-Chi who had come back. An old morbid
ambition for greatness had disappeared. Kind, friendly and
understanding, he went around ready to serve and help even the
youngest of the fraternity. His regular hours of meditation, his
skill and energy, as well as the joy and inwardness which marked
his participation in worship, infected them all. It seemed as if a
new spirit had entered the monastery. In October Miao-Chi was
appointed a regular *fa-shih* with the task of starting courses for
young Buddhist monks in Formosa, and he was appointed leader
of literary activities in the monastery as well. As his special helpers
in teaching he was given brothers Ta-Hsuan and Man-T'u, both
born in Formosa and both well-educated men of religious disposition. With them he began to prepare the work and it was not
long before these three developed a firm friendship. Both of these
men had been apprehensive of Miao-Chi's return because they
were afraid of being put into the shade and had already planned to
leave. This intention they now abandoned as Miao-Chi took them
into all his plans, at the same time letting them understand that he
placed the highest value upon their abilities and devotion.

By Lunar New Year 1924 enough young and well-educated
monks had been collected in Fa Yün Ssu for the work to begin.
A record of this occasion appeared in Miao-Chi's periodical
Asia's Light that began the following autumn. It read as follows:

> The opening of the first Buddhist Academy in Formosa took place
> recently. The Abbot introduced the master, Miao-Chi, who is in charge of
> the course, in these words, 'It will be evident to you that we are now ventur-
> ing to start this higher Buddhist Academy because my disciple Miao-Chi has
> returned after more than five years' study in Japan and China. He has used his
> time well and has graduated with distinction as *fa-shih* from T'ai-Hsü's well-
> known academy. I hereby install him as head of the Formosa Academy and
> I pray you all, students and fellow-teachers, to gather around him in con-
> fidence and respect.'

From Miao-Chi's speech the following extract is given:

> It is with great happiness and gratitude that I begin this work among
> Buddhist youth in Formosa, although I am acutely aware of the responsibility
> and of my own limitations. At the same time I have a strong sense of the
> importance of this task. Never has our island more needed the power and
> warmth of religion than now. New education, inventions and modernization
> can only become a blessing if they are made parts of a deep religious life.
> Man cannot by any magic way create religious life; it grows mysteriously in
> the hidden world of the heart. You will thus understand that the aim of our
> course here at Fa Yün Ssu is something much more than to gather knowledge

and become eloquent masters who can perform in glittering mass robes and with the gestures and manners of a scholar. The aim is, through studies, devotions, meditation and fellowship, to enter into a deeper understanding of life and the clear realization of the special calling of heaven for service to mankind. The aim is to become a *bodhisattva* who sees and thinks clearly and whose joy it is to serve and help one's fellow men in the spiritual and temporal realms. We have the pleasure of seeing about fifty young men present to-day chosen from Formosa's temples and monasteries. What would it not mean to our beloved island if all you young men made up your minds to use these two years for thorough preparation for a life of service! Another thing I must add, and that is the importance of teachers and students being united in full understanding. None of us is perfect; let us therefore prepare to help one another. Let us not be afraid of "losing face" as we prepare for the service of a *bodhisattva* so that the wheel of salvation can operate in the hearts of men.

Such a speech had never before been heard in Formosa. Many were deeply moved, others were shocked; but all agreed that a new and important era had begun.

It was not only the fifty students who sat enthusiastically at Miao-Chi's feet; several of the officials of the monastery, the Abbot, Deputy Abbot, fellow-teachers and even a number of visiting pilgrims were frequently to be seen in the audience. The hall they were using became too small, so that they had to move into the temple hall itself. The audience was particularly large when Miao-Chi lectured on comparative religion, where he was obviously in his element.[1] No less well attended were informal lectures when Miao-Chi reported upon his impressions and experiences during his visit to Japan and China. Much time was spent on correspondence too. A number of friends in China and Japan kept him informed on developments within Buddhist circles. They wanted his views on various questions or they asked for articles and statements for Buddhist periodicals which were springing up in various places in the East during those years.

Altogether it proved a rich and profitable time, and the academy work continued undisturbed by riots and conflicts that have so often upset education in China. There was no question of political disturbance or intrigue because the Japanese ruled with an iron hand and had their security agents watching the population and particularly the students. Among these young men were some, of course, who even under these favourable conditions remained

[1] It is from Man-T'u's oral recollections that the author has obtained most of the information on Miao-Chi's activities as teacher, lecturer and journalist.

unimpressed; but they were few. The majority practised their private devotions earnestly.

Now and then Miao-Chi took the whole group with him on mountain walks and he was not satisfied until everyone had found a spot where he could collect his thoughts. Now and then he took small groups with him on travels in the district as frequent invitations reached him to take part in meetings in various parts of Formosa. In this way the young men became bound to him in a unique way. He became at one and the same time elder brother, teacher and friend to every individual.

In the spring of 1925 the Abbot decided to send an application to the Council of Elders for Miao-Chi to be appointed an assistant abbot at Fa Yün Monastery. He himself had not expected this; still, he appreciated the honour because his position would be strengthened in the chief monastery and indeed throughout the island. The application was approved and Miao-Chi obtained thereby many new opportunities. It became necessary to undertake frequent tours of inspection, and Miao-Chi, who always took his duties seriously, obtained a true picture of conditions in the Buddhist communities. That picture was not bright. The numerous small Buddhist temples spread around in town and country laboured under economic difficulties, and for this reason several of them had been driven into connection with obscure people who made money from wrong-doing and vice. Many of the monks were vicious and ignorant and worship was in some places degraded by superstition and greed.

It was Miao-Chi's duty to reform these conditions and, open and courageous as he was, he energetically embarked upon his task. He made many enemies even if he won the esteem of right-thinking people.

It was on the basis of these experiences that he felt driven to found the Buddhist Reform Association. The aims came out clearly in a leading article in *Asia's Light*:

1. To preach and practise Mahayana Buddhism in its greatness and purity.
2. To free Buddhist communities from those monks who live in vice and corruption and who are unwilling to be converted.
3. To fight and eradicate superstition.
4. To help young people who have the will and ability to become socially useful.
5. To adopt energetic and broadly-planned measures for economic and social progress in Formosa.

6. To awaken the population of Formosa to an understanding of their privileges and duties.

7. To level out artificial and damaging class distinctions and lead men on to communal well-being.

Miao-Chi placed his programme before the authorities and obtained their approval; then, during a meeting in the capital, in a branch temple of Fa Yün Ssu called Lung Shan Ssu, the Association was founded with Miao-Chi as president. The meeting was packed. Some expressed their warm and whole-hearted approval but many signed as members because it would not look well to stand aloof. They consoled themselves with the thought that, as in so many Chinese reform associations, the decisions would only remain on paper. However these people had not taken into account that this time it was Miao-Chi who was leader. He felt that it was his duty to put such decisions into effect at home, namely, in the chief monastery itself.

Now it had long been an open secret that two monks who occupied important positions there had sunk deeply into dishonesty and loose living. Their names were Wu-Hsin and Rü-Hui. The Abbot realized that it was necessary to do something but hesitated, knowing that these two monks had considerable influence in the capital. They had already on several occasions shown ill will towards Miao-Chi and tension grew when they saw how fearlessly he procceded with his plans. Now that the Reform Association had been founded it came to a final breach. All the other monks in the monastery had signed as members and only Wu-Hsin and Rü-Hui stood aloof. There is an old practice in Chinese monasteries that the Abbot should deliver a short speech or exhortation at breakfast time. He concludes by saying that if anyone has something on his mind this is the opportunity to speak out. One morning as the Abbot ended his speech and asked the usual question, Miao-Chi stood up and said: "It is a well-known fact that everyone here has gladly entered into the work of cleansing and elevating our Buddhist community in Formosa. Only Wu-Hsin and Rü-Hui stand aloof. We all know the reason; they have long followed a course of dishonesty and loose living. We have exhorted them to repentance and conversion but without result. There is now no other course of action than this to make our monastery the pure and radiant place we all long for; I therefore propose that these two be removed immediately from our midst."

The Abbot in his lofty chair coughed uneasily. He was grateful as well as shocked, but remembering his duty he said in a low voice, "Is there anyone who has anything to add?" Nobody spoke a word; they knew very well that there could be no excuse and the outcome was clear. That same day the two monks left. Everybody drew sighs of relief but at the same time realized that Miao-Chi had now made two implacable enemies who would not rest until they had taken revenge.

20

Writer and Seeker

ATTEMPTS HAD BEEN made for years to encourage literary activity among the Buddhists of Formosa but nothing had been organized; it was all rather casual and spasmodic. Some teachers had edited their lectures, and a modest selection of popular writings on the Pure Land School was available in a number of temples and monasteries. Japanese monks had opened a Buddhist bookshop in Taipeh, the capital, but their publications were chiefly in Japanese and thus inaccessible to the great majority.

Miao-Chi was aware that a new effort must be made, and with his usual energy he threw himself into the task. He wrote a number of leaflets on the Pure Land viewpoint and edited one or two simple books on comparative religion. These writings obtained wide circulation in Formosa. No less important, in all the larger towns he organized literary associations. He founded such an association for Buddhist scholars with its centre in Lung Shan Ssu ("Dragon Mountain Temple") in Taipeh. Here a bookshop was opened for the sale of Buddhist literature. Most important, perhaps, was Formosa's first Buddhist periodical, *Ya Kuang* (*Asia's Light*).

For several years Miao-Chi had been thinking of this magazine, because, during his stay in China and Japan, he had seen the influence of such periodicals on modern cultural life. His magazine would become an excellent pulpit from which his message and plans for reform could reach a wider field. Still, Miao-Chi realized that it might prove a difficult undertaking under political conditions as they were in Formosa. He had to be prepared to take in a good deal of distasteful material for the benefit of the Japanese rulers who would scan every issue with argus eyes. Much tact and wisdom would be needed if he wished to steer clear of shoals. Chinese culture and violent Japanese nationalism tended to be focused together in Formosa. Miao-Chi took a realistic view of it all in spite of being thoroughly Chinese at heart. He had seen much of Chinese maladministration and could not fail to appreciate the order that had been established with a strong hand by the Japanese. He hoped, too, that the new wave of education and economic advance that was making itself felt perhaps offered liberty and security in the future. From his idealistic point of view he could see that both China and Japan had values of importance for the family of mankind. These values were tied primarily, he believed, to culture and religion, and here he had to include the whole of Asia, above all that notable centre of religion, India. He saw as if in a vision the religions and culture of Asia like a rising sun with healing in its rays. To Miao-Chi this sun was represented by sages such as Lao-tzu, Confucius, Chuang-tzu, Sakyamuni Buddha and, farther west, by the great *bodhisattva*, Jesus the Christ.

The vision settled into a definite picture, and this naturally became the cover design for his periodical: a map of Asia irradiated by a rising sun with the two characters "Ya Kuang" at the top. This was the interpretation that Miao-Chi put upon the cover. There were others, however, who read different meanings into it. Many Buddhists thought exclusively of Sakyamuni Buddha, of whom even a Western poet used the phrase "The light of Asia".[1] Others thought of Asia as represented by vigorous Japan, then expanding everywhere as Nippon ("Land of the Rising Sun"), and the symbol certainly was reminiscent of the Japanese national flag.

In the beautifully-produced first number, issued in the autumn of 1924, the main aim was stressed of awakening people in general and Buddhists in particular to the immense importance of religion. As a whole the tone was moderate. Miao-Chi thought it wise not to press forward too hastily at first. It was different with the numbers that followed. With constantly-increasing courage and power he took up questions that were topical, especially in the Buddhist world. The fiery zeal of the reformer was noticeable in every line. No wonder that the periodical created a good deal of sensation and that articles were reprinted not only in Japan and China but also in Java and Malaya.

At the beginning finance proved somewhat of a problem, and

[1] Cf. Edwin Arnold's poem on Sakyamuni, *The Light of Asia*.

it was only through generous gifts from wealthy lay Buddhists that the periodical could be kept going. By 1926 it had become so popular that self-support had been achieved. This was a great relief to Miao-Chi and his small circle of assistants. He still lived up at his beloved monastery, Fa Yün Ssu, but often travelled to the capital where a colleague, Hsü-Shan, looked after literary affairs in the branch temple. Instruction still occupied the greater part of his day so he perforce had to use the night hours for his steadily-increasing literary activity.

Shortly before New Year 1926 the first batch of students from the Academy graduated. Miao-Chi felt that he had reached a milestone, for on that day he was able to send out the first group of pioneers in the reform movement, young monks kindled by the same fire and willing to sacrifice and suffer for their fellow men. A new batch came in, this time comprising about seventy, which meant that Miao-Chi was gradually reaching the majority of Formosa's educated Buddhist young men.

Through the successive numbers of the periodical *Asia's Light* his journeys can be followed through the island. During these lecture tours Miao-Chi founded a number of study circles and Buddhist associations. He had many uplifting experiences when he was able to see the fire of revival spreading amongst young and old. There were also many hard tasks to undertake, such as cleaning up corruption. Miao-Chi's most profitable hours were spent among lay Buddhists, and he noticed how frequently the so-called evangelical tendency of the Pure Land doctrine brought out a longing for deliverance and renewal. Yet his own world of thought was more and more filled with doubt and anguish. Even concerning the Pure Land, with all its glowing prayers and poems about Amitabha and the power of faith, he could not escape the fact that its entire foundation was weak and mythical. He knew (what most people did not) that the teaching about Amitabha had no historical foundation. He knew that all this talk of the "All-Father" was simply a construction of thought that might be good enough as a working hypothesis but lacked the spirit of a real person. Thus it came about that the more the laity gathered around him in gratitude and expectancy the more he felt fear arise within his own heart. Here he was posing as a spiritual leader but within himself there was doubt and insecurity.

During such periods, beset by doubt and anguish, it was a help to come back to regular teaching in the chief monastery. There he found many tasks that helped to keep his spirit balanced, and there he had time to concentrate upon his favourite study of comparative religion. More and more clearly he became aware that something more than a mere impulse to study was impelling him. He was a seeker and must find a secure historical basis for religious faith. He became aware too that heaven had given him special abilities as a revivalist preacher, and he had felt the thrill of facing large masses as a heaven-sent messenger, but lately a dreadful fear had prompted new questions. Was his message straightforward? Was he really able to lead men upwards? In this plight he decided to spend more time in meditation. He had several literary tasks lying waiting and with these in mind the problem became still more serious. The result was that his night's sleep, already short, became further reduced. He had to search and ponder and think as never before.

So the years 1926 and 1927 passed. The second course was coming to a close. Everyone knew that the Academy had done excellent work. The young men returned to their home monasteries full of eagerness and enthusiasm and for many the stay had meant inward renewal. Gradually it appeared that the Buddhist community in Formosa was unrecognizable in comparison with what it used to be. The seed was growing in men's hearts, even through those difficult years when the leader himself was passing through the mists of uncertainty.

Now that most of the young monks in Formosa had had opportunity of taking the course it became possible for the Academy to cease activity for some time. From 1928 Miao-Chi became free from the exacting teaching work and gave all his time to preaching and literary activity. It became clear that he ought to move his place of work to Taipeh, the capital, where he was solemnly installed as abbot of Lung Shan Ssu ("Dragon Mountain Temple").

His colleagues, Man-T'u and Ta-Hsuan, returned from a visit to China during the last months of 1927 and spent some time with Miao-Chi. It did him good to sit with them and exchange memories of China. They had much to tell him, especially about Nanking where both of them had taken a course at Ou-Yang Ching Wu's Buddhist Academy. During their stay in Nanking they had made repeated visits to the Ching Feng Shan[1] Brother-

---

[1] Conducted by the author for the Christian instruction of Buddhist monks.

hood and were now full of enthusiasm for what they had seen and heard. Man-T'u produced a New Testament and a book on the essence of religion that we had just issued. Their experiences gave rise to long conversations on the nature of Christianity. It appeared that Man-T'u had become interested in such questions and was now an eager student of the Bible. Neither was Ta-Hsuan uninfluenced, but he mostly kept his thoughts to himself. Ta-Hsuan was, however, very interested in hearing his two friends talk about the person of Christ and Church ritual.

Miao-Chi constantly turned over in his mind all that he had heard of the Christian Brotherhood in China. If only he too could visit the place, or at least be able to meet one of its leaders!

21

Wilderness of Doubt

IT WAS ABOUT Christmas, 1927, that Miao-Chi took up residence in the island capital, Taipeh. His name was well known and esteemed there as he had often spent weeks in Lung Shan Ssu in connection with literature work and had given lectures in the monastery. Now he was to become permanently connected with the place as abbot.

The arrival of Miao-Chi brought life and activity into a temple hitherto relatively quiet, since he brought with him a staff of his best students. Soon he and Hsü-Shan had arranged a modern bookshop and one room was converted into a reading-room. Buddhist scholars gathered there to scan the latest literature. In the mornings numbers of lay people, men and women, came to worship and several desired personal interviews.

During his academy teaching Miao-Chi had given the young monks intensive instruction on how to conduct mass in a solemn and dignified manner. This resulted in more people gathering for service than ever before. Especially popular were the masses in the Pure Land style at sunset and these linked up with public lectures in the evening. In his lectures Miao-Chi dealt with religious and social subjects, and in consequence numbers of the upper classes began to find their way to the temple. Soon a larger association, the O-Mi-T'o-Fu Society, was founded with the aim of spreading the light of Amitabha so as to reach all departments of life. This society became of importance to many people in the capital and after some months branches grew up in several large towns. Editorial and other literary work occupied much of Miao-Chi's time and often the night had to be used too. He could not get around to visit societies and branches as frequently as he wished, but he found an alternative. One hour each day was spent in "team education", that is, he trained a chosen group of students in the difficult art of reaching individuals through personal work. These students were then sent out, two or three together, in place of their leader. Many interesting records of their experiences were published in *Asia's Light* and they give a vivid impression of the new wind that was blowing from Dragon Mountain.

It was chiefly in the city of Taipeh that the breeze of revival was felt. Here the evening meetings were often prolonged into after-meetings and when these were over there was nearly always a little group waiting for personal interviews with the master. Many of these seekers after truth insisted upon becoming his personal disciples. He tried to restrain them but the demand became so strong that he had to give in, and after some months the number of these personal disciples amounted to several hundreds.

Among Miao-Chi's hearers were some young men who had no financial means of continuing their professional training or studies. These came and sought his help. Many poor and needy people begged his assistance too. With his deep social interest Miao-Chi regarded it as his duty to do all within his power for these folk. Among his circle of acquaintances were several prominent and affluent people and by their aid he succeeded in helping many to achieve economic independence. Gifts were poured into the temple as never before, and Miao-Chi persuaded the Council of Elders to agree that a certain percentage should be put aside for the needy and destitute.

From time to time deputations and visitors arrived from cultural and religious circles in China and Japan. It became a matter of course that they should visit Lung Shan Ssu, now the centre of cultural and religious life in Formosa. Government authorities had become aware of the great influence Miao-Chi exerted and he was frequently called in at various receptions and festivities. His eloquence and the ease with which he mastered various languages came to his aid. Without difficulty he could speak in Mandarin, the Amoy and Hakka dialects, as well as in Japanese. The Council of Elders and leaders of Fa Yün Ssu were, of course, very pleased with Miao-Chi as an administrator, for never had Lung Shan Ssu brought so rich an income to the common treasury. At the same time many shook their heads anxiously over his plans for reform. Some leaders began to express a fear that this unusual monk might soon wear himself out under heavy pressure of work. There were also several conservative monks and laymen who noticed with increasing disapproval how articles in *Asia's Light*, as well as his speeches and lectures, included more and more ideas from sources obviously not Buddhist. They did not realize the full truth of the matter. They had no notion of the inner anguish and uncertainty in Miao-Chi's mind. Only Man-T'u, his understanding friend, noticed the trouble that showed itself in his face.

Through his religious studies and steady meditation Miao-Chi had entered more and more into a wilderness of doubt. He had begun to doubt whether Buddhism as a system really offered a solution to life's deepest problems and the innermost needs of the human soul. Theoretically he was convinced that faith and self-dedication were the most important things in religious life, and he had concentrated for some years on the ideals of the Pure Land School, but he was now realizing that the foundations of the Pure Land system were not only misty and insecure but positively misleading. With increasing clearness he now saw that such a "constructed" way of salvation, however inspiring, can never provide the certainty of man's salvation. As a conscientious scholar he knew that it was historically impossible to suppose that Sakyamuni Buddha, who according to the oldest and most reliable Buddhist sources refused to accept the thought of salvation through a divine mediator, should at last have given way to popular opinion so as to regard the mythical Amitabha as Universal Saviour and King of the Western Paradise. Yet this was exactly what the Pure Land's two classical writings, the Amitabha Scripture and the Sakyamuni Scripture, proclaimed. Miao-Chi knew very well the intellectual toil given by learned Buddhists over centuries in order to reconcile these opposing ideas. The Pure Land view was always explained as a useful working hypothesis to make it easier for believers, so that in due course they would awake and see the whole Amitabha conception as an inspiring symbol of man's initial experience of Nirvana (self-realization, not extinction). Now that he was a recognized leader of revival these doubts came over him like a chilly breath and took all power and cheerfulness out of him. Again and again when he saw the expectant faces before him or when anxious folk came to him privately he felt an urge to run away and hide in shame.

Miao-Chi remembered what Man-T'u had recently told him about the Brotherhood at Ching Feng Shan, where men spoke and sang of salvation through faith in a divine mediator sent from God. This mediator was not Amitabha or any other mythical *bodhisattva* but the historic Jesus, whose triumphant gospel had been so faithfully recorded in the New Testament. Miao-Chi longed to tear himself loose from this doubting existence and take a trip to Ching Feng Shan, or at any rate meet one of its leaders. The strain became almost unbearable. Should he run away? Perhaps the only thing left for him was to end his life? But that would be cowardly. In despair Miao-Chi threw himself upon his face not in front of an altar of Buddha but in the middle of his cell. A sigh and a prayer escaped him, "O Heaven, have mercy, and send a teacher who can lead me onward to the light!" All this happened during the night of March 5, 1928.

22

Illumination at Last

ON THE FOLLOWING morning, March 6, I visited Miao-Chi at Lung Shan Ssu. It was my first visit to Formosa.

I had had a strong feeling that I had been guided by God to this encounter, and when we met the same appeared to be the case with Miao-Chi, only to him it was not the personal God but rather the hidden powers of *karma* that were operating. After studying my visiting-card he grasped my hand and smilingly exclaimed, "At last the day has come when our good *karma* has brought us together! I have heard so much about you and your work and often wondered when we should meet. It is really wonderful because I have just been thinking so much about your Christian Brotherhood."

Chinese, and especially Buddhists, have a strong belief in the existence of a mysterious contact or affinity between certain people. This affinity is thought to be the result of previous existences often hundreds of years earlier. This is especially the case where good *karma*, or merit, has been accumulated over a long period. Buddhists call this phenomenon *yuan*. Perhaps most commonly known is the saying, "Those with mutual affinity will meet though a thousand miles apart; those without it will never meet though living in the same street." This mutual feeling of a holy destiny proved from the very outset to be an ever-increasing inspiration in our conversations. His sincere and frank remarks made it easier for me to express what I felt. Formalities of tea-drinking were quickly got through, and after a few minutes, when we were sitting together in his cell, it was possible for me to speak.

"I too have a strong feeling," I said, "that there is something providential in our meeting just now, and that we shall be of help and blessing to one another. Before entering a monastery I always have a time of silence, praying that I may meet such people as have been prepared in some measure for understanding and receiving the message of the Kingdom of God. I pray for wisdom so that my words may become a blessing from above. This I did before entering your temple to-day especially because I felt the urgency of finding a man who, through personal experience of the living God, could become a missionary to Buddhists in Formosa."

It was plain to see that these words had found their way to Miao-Chi's heart for he said, "Do you really believe that it is God who has led us to meet? Do you Christians believe that there is a God who can and will reveal His will? Does the Bible really say that men can hear the voice of God and be guided by Him whenever they are in difficulties? I know that you think in terms of a personal God but to us that is very difficult to understand. If God is personal then He must be subject to limitations and therefore no longer God."

Thus question after question arose expressing the doubts and tormenting problems which had been gathering in his mind over a long time. I sensed that here was a man not interested in asking questions for the sake of discussion but because he yearned for true understanding.

Although Miao-Chi possessed a Bible and had met people who in one way or another had had some contact with Christians, he himself had never talked with a Christian missionary or other Christians about the faith, so it was all the more wonderful to see how the Spirit of God, through the events of his life and by quiet work within, had prepared his mind for our meeting.

I said, "Let us begin with your first question, asking if we Christians can approach God with our problems and difficulties fully convinced that God will answer. I can assure you this will always be the case if we sincerely wish to live according to His will. The answer will come, if not at once then at some time when He thinks best. You ask further if our Bible has anything to say about this. Yes, definitely. Even in the Old Testament times there were some of the prophets who could say with Isaiah,[1] 'Thine ears shall hear a word behind thee, saying, This is the way, walk ye in it, when ye turn to the right hand, and when ye turn to the left'. Above all, we find it expressed in the New Testament.

[1] Isa. 30: 21.

Jesus said[1] 'Ask, and it shall be given you, seek, and ye shall find, knock, and it shall be opened unto you.' We read that the apostles during their missionary travels listened for the voice of God before making final decisions. They had already planned a journey according to human deliberations, but in testing their plan in the light of God they realized that the Spirit of Jesus, which is also the Holy Spirit of God, clearly showed them another way and with far-reaching results.

"Let us read this together," I said, "in the Acts:[2]

> 'And they went through the region of Phrygia and Galatia, having been forbidden by the Holy Spirit to speak the word in Asia. And when they reached Mysia, they tried to enter Bithynia; but the Spirit of Jesus would not permit them.'

"Note what happened as a result of that change *en route*; it was a result for which we in Europe thank God, because the Gospel was preached for the first time on the European mainland. Further we read:[3]

> 'And passing by Mysia they came down to Troas. There a vision appeared to Paul in the night; a man of Macedonia stood beseeching him and saying, Come over to Macedonia and help us. As a result of the vision we immediately tried to go into Macedonia, concluding that God had called us to preach the Gospel unto them.'

"See how important it is to listen to the voice of God," I said to Miao-Chi, "and follow the guidance of His Spirit. We do not always expect to see visions in our dreams or receive supernatural revelation of what the will of God is, but we know that those who earnestly wait upon the Lord will be given adequate guidance as though they heard 'a word behind them saying, This is the way, walk ye in it'. Both you and I feel that we have been led to meet to-day, only for you this must seem to be a result of impersonal powers of destiny, while for me it is a token of our Heavenly Father's gracious leading."

Here Miao-Chi broke in eagerly saying, "Yes, that is true, and what a difference it makes! How I wish that I could see it as you do, because that would mean a new and secure foundation for my whole life. I have studied our Chinese classics and often felt that when the sages, such as Confucius, Mencius, Moti and Wang Yang-Ming, reached so far in insight and personal devotion

---

[1] Matt. 7: 7.   [2] Acts 16: 6–7.   [3] Acts 16: 8–10

the reason was that T'ien ('Heaven') or Shang Ti ('The Exalted Ruler') to them was really what you Christians mean by speaking of a personal God. On the other hand, through studies in Buddhism, I have been led to think that all that is personal must necessarily be subject to limitation. The idea of a personal God has therefore receded into the background of my thinking.

"I felt," continued Miao-Chi, "that I had to concentrate instead on something which can be said to be divine, even though not in a personal way, namely the self-existent ideas which lie behind reality and reflect themselves vaguely in our lives and in the life of the universe (Chinese, *chen-ru*). Only he who has become per-fectly enlightened, a Buddha, reflects reality and is able to compre-hend it in its fulness. He has become a *ru-lai*, that is to say, the fundamental pattern of life has become personalized in him. For this reason a Buddha stands far above gods and saints. He should be in no need of a god as he himself shares in the inner life of and is at one with the universe. In spite of this there is among us Buddhists a desperate need of something more tangible or, if you like, more personal.

"I must tell you," said Miao-Chi, "that I came into contact with Christians in an indirect and unusual way some years ago. The first time was in Japan when on Koyasan I saw the magnificent replica of the Nestorian Tablet. Its profound thoughts have, more than anything else, created in me a longing for a full understand-ing of the Christian idea of God. Later, through Professor Suzuki's lectures, I was led to realize that Christ has meant some-thing unique to the world. Through the same esteemed master I was introduced to the man who has meant so much for social progress in Japan, Tenko Nishida. To him Christianity has been an important source of inspiration because it was his reading of the life of Francis of Assisi which opened his eyes to social problems. And now I meet you! There must be a mysterious connection in all this."

Again it was my turn to speak. I felt responsibility and happiness now that we had come to the deepest and most fundamental questions. I prayed again and again, "O Lord, lead thou my thoughts and give the words wherewith to express them!" Here is a short rendering of what I said:

"I fully understand your difficulties. They have been felt more or less clearly at all times and in all places. We Christians feel that it is not easy to use the word 'personal' and 'personality' in describing God, who naturally must be above any limitation implied in that word. Especially is it difficult in Chinese where the word 'personal' always suggests the human sphere. Once we have understood this difficulty it is easier to remember that we here use the word in a higher sense, excluding the notion of limitation. Some people have found it helpful to add 'supra' to the word 'personal', thus emphasizing the meaning of a personality without human limitations.

"Let me make it clear that it is from Jesus that we come to a real understanding of God. There is a general revelation of God in the world which we share together with the most enlightened in all the higher religions. It gives us an important basis for our knowledge of God, mainly through observation of creation and the remarkable regularity which characterizes nature in its operations. Think of what Confucius, Mencius and Moti have said about these things. Consider how clearly the Eastern sages have indicated those moral laws that lie behind everything and their more or less clear reflection in the conscience of man. We gratefully recognize that God 'left not Himself without witness'[1] but we can see that this general revelation is insufficient. It is most clearly confirmed by the fact that many of our best thinkers wonder whether there is a personal, or shall we better say, suprapersonal God behind the universe, or whether there is only a basic pattern or abstract idea. If one has only nature or the manifestations of nature to lean upon, then the idea of God becomes a synthesis of the good and the beautiful, but the picture is disturbed by disharmony and brutality. It shows outlines and intentions of a most attractive cosmos, and yet outlines and intentions of dreadful chaos too."

I pointed out to Miao-Chi some of the main teachings of Jesus. "First, God is Spirit. Therefore Jesus says,[2] 'They that worship Him must worship Him in spirit and in truth'. In spite of God being Spirit, and therefore above all limitations of time and space, He is at the same time our Father. That is Christ's chosen expression for God. We may say that the main purpose of Christ's teaching and activity was to reveal to man that God is our Father and that He loves us in spite of all our misery and sin. This does not imply any limitation of God. One of Christ's greatest apostles, Paul,

[1] Acts 14: 17.　　　　[2] John 4: 24.

says, 'One God and Father of all, who is over all and through all and in all'.[1] As our Father and the Father of the universe He is the all-pervading and all-including, 'in whom we live and move and have our being'.[2]

"In John's writings is a comprehensive expression for God and His nature, namely, 'God is love'. This expression is used twice in the First Epistle of John.[3] It is so important that we must read it together. Let us first take the 16th and then the 8th verse:

'And we know and have believed the love which God hath toward us. God is love; and he that abideth in love abideth in God, and God abideth in him. He that loveth not knoweth not God; for God is love.'

"This then is the nature of God. Love is the fountain from which springs all that constitutes His divine nature, holiness, righteousness, mercy and wisdom. It is the foundation of the most holy and profound in our Christian faith. This, I imagine, you have heard something about before, but new light is shed upon it whenever we speak of love as the fundamental property of God's nature. I think of that word of Scripture which one of the stalwarts of the Church, Martin Luther, has called 'the little Bible', namely John 3: 16:

'For God so loved the world, that He gave his only begotten Son, that whosoever believeth in him should not perish, but have eternal life.'

"You will understand that behind this word of Scripture is discernible the very heart of the Christian faith, the atonement effected on Calvary, when Jesus gave His life a ransom for many.

"I look forward to further talks with you on this subject because it is so great and so fundamental.

"Now let us take up the next point you mentioned regarding the fundamental meaning of life (Chinese, *chen-ru*). It was interesting to hear that through this Buddhist term you had found an expression that could help you to anticipate something of the divine. True, there is a certain connection here because the Christian view also contains the idea that God is the foundation of life. The Greeks, through their greatest religious thinker, Plato, attained to a similar belief. He spoke of a spiritual 'world of ideas' which lies behind all external manifestations. He did not stop there: he linked this spiritual world with the divine to mean the

[1] Eph. 4: 6.   [2] Acts 17: 28.   [3] 1 John 4.

highest intelligence and will. Plato tried hard to free the idea of God from human limitations.

"There are indications in Buddhist thought that point beyond impersonal qualifications; for instance, the conception of trinity as developed in the Hua Yen Ching (*Avatamsaka Sutra*). There it is described as the fundamental plan with three important aspects; 1) '*ti*', the body or model, 2) '*hsiang*', the image made manifest through revelation, and 3) '*yung*' the realization or activity. For us Christians too the divine is made manifest in three different forms. We call it the doctrine of the Trinity, and it contains some of the most exalted thoughts in the Christian faith. Of God, as the foundation of life, the New Testament says He is 'dwelling in light unapproachable'.[1] Compare the saying in the Fourth Gospel.[2] 'No man hath seen God; the only begotten Son, who is in the bosom of the Father, he hath declared him'. There is something in God that is hidden but God has also revealed Himself, and in doing this He has taken on an 'image' in his Son, the only-begotten. About him Scripture says that he is 'the true image of God'. Again and again this designation is used for Jesus. (Compare Heb. 1: 3, 'He who is the effulgence of his glory, and the very image of his substance'. See also Col. 1: 15, 'He who is the image of the invisible God'.) Then there is the third aspect, the Son, Jesus Christ, who now acts through the Spirit after having concluded his earthly task. Thus the living Christ is present amongst us, acting through the Spirit."

*   *   *

This first conversation with Miao-Chi was the beginning of our friendship. It broke down the barriers and filled us both with a wonderful feeling of urgency and promise. We decided that time would be used to the best advantage by meeting every morning and afternoon, sometimes in the temple and sometimes in the Canadian Mission where I was staying.

During the afternoon of that first day, at my invitation, Miao-Chi began to give an account of his life. This he continued during our conversation on the following afternoon. I wrote down the details as completely as possible because I soon realized that this material would prove of the utmost value in the future. He showed great confidence in me by placing some of his diaries in my hands.

[1] 1 Tim. 6: 16.   [2] John 1: 18.

The morning hours were used for Bible studies and talks on the Christian faith. I had brought with me copies of Luther's Catechism. Some of these hours really became informal cate-chumen classes. One whole morning was spent in going through the text of the Nestorian Tablet that Miao-Chi had copied. After some time it became natural for us to begin and end these talks with prayer and a short meditation. Great was my joy when Miao-Chi began to take audible part in prayer. The first time he prepared the wording on a piece of paper but later he prayed freely. Miao-Chi's first prayer was very short but full of meaning and well formed. It ran:

> Holy God, Thou who through Jesus Christ hast revealed Thyself to man-kind, I thank Thee and offer praise to Thee because I too am allowed to come under the power of Thy Spirit and learn to know Thee. I thank Thee that at this time Thou hast brought about my meeting with this teacher from the West according to Thy eternal purpose. Bless us as we now kneel in Thy sight, and fulfil Thy will and Thy work in us.

During our talks on the first article, about God as Creator and Upholder of the Universe, Miao-Chi put forward problems and difficulties which are typical of Buddhists when they come into touch with the Christian faith. Here is a summary of our talks on this subject.

Miao-Chi said that he had never felt satisfied with Buddhist doctrines about creation. On the one hand it is maintained that matter is *maya* ("emptiness" or "illusion"); on the other, that matter is eternal. Hence there can be no real creation but only evolution as well as involution. Buddhists think of matter as consisting of "the four main elements" that constitute the material world—air, fire, water and earth. Through four long periods of time, coming-into-existence, stagnation, disintegration and annihilation, the universe passes through an endless circle of evolution and involution while the elements become mingled. This will continue as long as there is any ignorance or craving for life (*avidya* and *tanha*) which, from a spiritual point of view, according to Buddhism, constitute the main cause for the coming into existence of living beings, for individuation and for the chain of suffering through an endless succession of birth and death (*samsara*).

The genesis of the world and the suffering of mankind are thus closely linked together because it is through the seeds of ignorance,

I

and those of craving or desire, that matter becomes condensed and creates different forms of existence according to the law of *karma* (consequences of our actions). Thus, life on this planet, with ignorance as its fundamental cause, becomes something that can only be deplored.

To Miao-Chi this explanation of life's origin was unacceptable; he felt that it ran counter to man's inmost feelings and instincts. Nevertheless it was difficult for him to follow the Christian thought of an all-loving and almighty God as the creator of the universe; so much evil and chaos in the world seemed to exclude any possibility of a perfect source.

I pointed out to Miao-Chi that according to the nature of things it is impossible for man to give an exhaustive and satis-factory solution of these questions, and they are closely linked with the problem of evil's origin, the existence of free will and the question whether dualism or monism is the final word. At the same time I tried to show him that to those who try to see reality in the light of their faith in Christ a new understanding is given regarding these riddles. I proceeded:

"What then is the view of the world and man held by Christ and His first disciples? First, that both man and his world belong to God. God is the Creator and Upholder, who 'maketh his sun to rise on the evil and on the good, and sendeth rain on the just and on the unjust'.[1] To Jesus, God is the Heavenly Father who 'knoweth that ye have need of all these things'.[2]

"Here we have the same view as in that wonderful hymn of creation which the spiritual leaders of the Jewish people com-posed from their ancient traditions and which they placed at the beginning of the Bible.[3] This hymn in praise of the Creator has, as its significant refrain, 'God saw everything that he had made, and lo, it was very good'. Here, as you see, there is a decided contrast between Buddhism and Christianity; on the one hand, decided pessimism, on the other, jubilant optimism.

"According to Buddhism the world and mankind have come into existence by a regrettable accident caused by ignorance and desire. According to Christianity there is purpose behind it all. This is only one side of the matter. The Christian faith knows something of the tragic side; there has been a fall, a catastrophe in the history of man. This too the spiritual leaders of the Jews

[1] Matt. 5: 45.   [2] Matt. 6: 32.   [3] Gen. 1: 1–2: 3.

rendered in a pictorial and dramatic way. It stands in Scripture side by side with the epic of our creation, and the effect by contrast is therefore much greater.[1] Jesus and his disciples saw the world not only as God's possession but peopled with beings who have fallen. Man has become like a lost sheep. The terrible dualism which has entered life is described in the words 'we know that we are of God, and the whole world lieth in wickedness'.[2]

"Thus Christianity," I maintained, "knows something of pessimism too and has been forced to labour under the problem of dualism, but let us remember that the final goal is not dualism and that the deepest note in the Christian faith is not pessimism but optimism. For God promises to make all things new. And the Apostle Paul says that the great goal will be reached through God becoming all in all.[3]

"You must understand," I pointed out to Miao-Chi, "that I am not saying that Christianity explains all riddles. The basic problem concerning the origin of evil cannot be solved completely by us Christians but I can testify from my experience that through faith in Christ an answer is given to some of the riddles of life. We anticipate that they will become clearer the more we enter into His life and light. Meaning thus comes into the facts of human existence. We are hopeful as we advance and take our places within God's Kingdom. It becomes a privilege to be a human being. Christ does not deliver us out of life but brings us into life."

[1] Gen. 3.   [2] 1 John 5: 19.   [3] 1 Cor. 15: 28.

23

The Great Decision

FOR ME IT was a fascinating experience to see how Miao-Chi progressed, step by step under the guidance of the Holy Spirit, to a decisive "break through" into the glorious liberty of the sons of God. In the terminology of the Apostle Paul he was being "rescued from the dominion of darkness and transferred to the Kingdom of his beloved Son".[1]

One day at the end of our devotions Miao-Chi turned to me with shining eyes and said, "At this moment, and in the presence of God, I solemnly vow to devote my life to Christ." I knew that this was sincere. After the insight I had gained from his life story I realized that an irrevocable decision had been made. I also knew that in his unusually difficult position his full transference into the Kingdom of God's beloved Son would mean enduring several more battles and much suffering. This I mentioned to him, but added at the same time, "I know you will be obedient to the Spirit of God. I am sure that all will be well eventually. Remember that God has given us sources of power in prayer, in the Bible and in Christian fellowship, so I beg you to seek earnestly the fellowship of the Church of God." This he promised to do.

After some days Miao-Chi arranged a series of public lectures for Buddhists and Christians. He settled arrangements very quickly and large audiences assembled. He chaired these meetings and acted as my translator from Mandarin. After three years on the mainland of China he spoke Mandarin fluently and could reproduce the contents of my address in Japanese, Hakka or in the Amoy dialect. A more skilful translator I have never met. It was significant that when he translated my description of mission work

1 Col. 1: 13.

amongst Buddhists and about our life in the Brotherhood Miao-Chi always used the "we" form, thus including himself. In other words, he felt that he was already one with us.

For the rest of the time we visited Chinese and Japanese temples together. In the company of Miao-Chi I was a welcome guest everywhere and many interesting talks ensued wherever we went. I should very much have liked him to accompany me in my trip through Formosa but his responsibilities in the capital were then too great. We had to be content with making plans for the time when he would be free and able to devote himself entirely to a task which was dawning upon him as his life's greatest work, the preaching of the Gospel of the Kingdom. He spoke to me of the possibility of establishing an affiliated branch of our Christian Brotherhood in Formosa. With that purpose in view he took me to see several Japanese and Chinese priests. On my side I had the pleasure of introducing him to Canadian missionaries and Chinese Church leaders in Taipeh as a brother who had decided for Christ. I told them that many things remained to be decided and that much tact and wisdom would be required on the part of all. Miao-Chi foresaw that it would inevitably come to a complete break with Buddhism. Yet he felt it to be his sacred duty to make use of his position in order to reach as many as possible inside the Buddhist community with a testimony of what Christ means. I could only answer, "Do what you believe to be your duty while constantly praying for the Spirit's guidance."

All too soon came the time for my departure. We both felt it very keenly, especially as Miao-Chi remarked how dark clouds were gathering around his horizon. Certain Buddhists were enraged against him for his reforming zeal and fight against corruption, and an attempt was being made to depose him from his position.

Before I left we had an unforgettable time of devotion together in my room in the Mission. On several occasions we had gone through our form of service together. After reading the seventeenth chapter of John's Gospel and offering free prayer we used our Brotherhood liturgy. Miao-Chi had expressed himself enthusiastically about this liturgy, in which a series of solemn phrases and expressions from China's oldest and most profound thoughts have been adapted and filled with a Christian content. He was untiring in quoting the words of dedication and the hymn with which we usually close a service in our Brotherhood.

Here is a rendering of the text of dedication that has proved such a blessing to many. It will give some impression of our common devotions and of my farewell meeting with Miao-Chi in the brilliant sunshine of that March day in 1928. This dedication does not replace traditional confessions of faith; it is rather an additional act of dedication for use when, gathered in our common faith and before the presence of God, we renew our resolve to go forward to the Kingdom. We all say the words of dedication together:

> With my whole heart I dedicate myself to God the Lord of the Universe, Creator of all life and Father of all mercy.
> With my whole heart I dedicate myself to Christ, the Reconciler for all our sins, the Restorer of our natures and the Revealer of God's wondrous plan of salvation.
> With my whole heart I dedicate myself to Him who embraces and pervades the universe, and who in every place has manifold ways to influence souls, even the pure and tranquilly-working Holy Spirit.

As a closing act comes the Hymn of Dedication sung to an old Buddhist chant:

> Bowed in dust at Thy feet I sing with confident faith, Lord Christ, True Saviour, and move onward towards the land of the living.
> Here this day I make my vow, confident and glad. In the power of Thy grace I move onward towards the living God.
> Thou who leadest mankind towards the heavenly home, grasp me with Thy hand and lead me safely onward into life.[1]

Then follow the Confession of Faith, Lord's Prayer and the Blessing.

[1] In the Chinese original this Hymn of Dedication consists of only one verse; this English translation is inevitably expanded somewhat.

24

Fire of Persecution

THE RESULTS OF Miao-Chi's radical change of mind soon began to be felt. The first was the stopping of all divination in the temple. It is the custom in Buddhist temples for people to throw dice and draw lots before the altar in order, they hope, to glimpse future events. Amongst educated and thoughtful monks this traffic is frowned upon but it nevertheless persists for the obvious reason that it is an important source of income.

Some members of the Council of Elders soon began to protest at the prohibition, but Miao-Chi referred them to the constitution of the Reform Association that opposed every form of superstition. This constitution all members of the Council of Elders had signed. This was only a preliminary skirmish on a negative issue; Miao-Chi felt that he must testify in a more positive way to his experience of new life and decided that this witness had to be given orally and in writing.

He asked for some weeks' leave. He felt that he needed silence, chiefly in order to gather his thoughts together upon the new life now opened to him with so much promise and yet so full of gravity. There was also another reason; Miao-Chi needed time to finish some articles introducing the fundamental truths of Christianity and he wished to prepare special lectures in order to explain his experiences openly. The application for leave was approved and he retired to a lonely little temple in the country. Every morning became a fruitful time of intense New Testament study, prayer and meditation. Afternoon hours were used for writing lecture notes and in preparing articles for *Asia's Light*. In Lung Shan Ssu the monks went about anxious and perplexed, and among Miao-Chi's disciples and the newly-awakened strange rumours began to circulate. What had come over their highly-esteemed master? He had not been himself since that time he acted as interpreter for the missionary.

After a month Miao-Chi returned. Anxiety amongst his friends began to lessen when they saw how healthy and happy he looked. There was a radiance in his face the like of which they had not seen before but there were deep lines graven too that told of inner tension.

Material for two issues of *Asia's Light* had been finished and Miao-Chi issued them at short intervals. In the first number appeared a long and instructive article on the nature of God. It was a complete reckoning with Buddhism. Miao-Chi demonstrated with acuteness and clarity the logical necessity of including the idea of God in the ancient religions of China, and from the pantheistic systems of Hinduism and Buddhism he selected various elements which, in a confused way, point to the idea of God. He then showed that only in the New Testament do men find the full solution where the living God is revealed through the unique *ru-lai* ("revealer"), Jesus the Christ. He is the perfect incarnation of God in nature, in will, and in heart.

In the following issues of *Asia's Light* Miao-Chi continued his exposition of the New Testament to draw a picture of Jesus, not only as the great Revealer but as the unique Saviour in whom the *bodhisattva* idea finds complete realization. The articles were a powerful Christian witness, and as a result many readers came to adopt an entirely new and positive standpoint towards Christianity. Nevertheless the articles called forth a storm of condemnation from conservative circles, and letters of protest flowed in, both to the Abbot and to members of the Council of Elders. Indignation in these circles grew stronger when Miao-Chi called a special meeting of his O-Mi-T'o-Fu Society. Formerly it was mainly Miao-Chi's friends and disciples who were accustomed to gather, but this time leading Buddhists came in large numbers precisely as Miao-Chi hoped.

From its beginning the lecture proved to be a personal witness and was listened to attentively. Most of Miao-Chi's friends and disciples were considerably moved, but many hearers felt it to be so new and revolutionary that they were quite at a loss. Some elders and lay Buddhists who had been closely attached to Miao-Chi were very shocked and some of them expressed their indignation by exclamations of protest. As a consequence the meeting broke up in confusion.

Miao-Chi gave a frank account of his religious development. Buddhism, he showed, had been a valuable help in forming an idea of life's inner meaning and had, as it were, given him a start in his quest for truth. Through Buddhism he had found the subject which eventually became his favourite, the study of comparative religion. This had helped him to come into closer contact with Christianity. During his stay in Japan and China he had, in what seemed a predestined way, again and again come into contact with Christ. He mentioned his experiences on Koyasan where he saw the replica of the Nestorian Tablet, his stirring conversations with Tenko Nishida and the spiritual inspiration he had received in reading of Francis of Assisi.

Regarding the various Buddhist schools he had learned to appreciate the views of the T'ien T'ai School and those of the School of Meditation but had come to see their decided limitations in that they excluded sources of power from faith and adoration. He had therefore found it necessary to concentrate on the Pure Land School that took cognizance of the most holy faculty of the human soul, faith. But here too he had run into difficulties because the more he inquired into and thought over these things the clearer it became that historic foundations for this popular way of salvation did not exist. This conclusion had caused him to fall into utter distress and agony of soul. Just as he was in direst need something remarkable had happened. Heaven itself had intervened, and who could be disobedient to such direct intervention? Quite unexpectedly there had come a Western missionary whom he knew about but with whom he had never before had any direct connection. Many of them had heard this man lecture. With this Western friend he had been able to speak freely, and a new understanding and peace had entered his life. This missionary had explained that what the Pure Land could only dimly perceive had been fulfilled in historical reality by the revelation of God's concern for mankind in Christ Jesus. Miao-Chi explained that before this he had read widely in the New Testament but from that day had taken up the study of this remarkable book very seriously. It was impossible to explain the flood of light and peace resulting from this study. He concluded, "It is my sincerest wish that you too, my friends, will concentrate upon this book so that you may find the only secure foundation for your hope in the future."

The very next day the number of his visitors had shrunk and even Hsü-Shan, his literary colleague, retired to the main monastery. The students who had followed Miao-Chi to Taipeh were divided; some returned to their respective temples, the majority voted to stand by their master through thick and thin. Study circles dissolved and only a few liberal-minded Buddhist scholars continued coming to the reading-room to study papers and periodicals. Letters poured in, some expressing anger and disgust, others sympathy. In the meantime Miao-Chi had found a place of strength and refuge in the Mission. As often as he could he attended meetings there and felt strengthened and blessed by divine worship on Sundays.

The rumour of Miao-Chi's conversion spread like wildfire throughout Formosa, and soon his two enemies, Wu-Hsin and Rü-Hui, heard of it. These two monks had not been idle. They had visited places where Miao-Chi lectured, and where, in his capacity of inspector, he had been compelled to discipline monks who led scandalous lives. With such disgruntled monks they prepared a list of accusations to use against Miao-Chi whenever occasion should arise. Now that occasion seemed to have come. They travelled quickly to Taipeh where they met two unscrupulous Buddhists. One was an elderly monk whose main source of income came from accepting bribes for the help he gave in unsavoury lawsuits. He had been educated as a lawyer and could therefore appear in court. The other was a Buddhist scholar named T'ang, who, through eloquence and cunning, had won a prominent place for himself in society. Both were distinguished by a bottomless love of money. They had succeeded in becoming members of the Council of Elders in Formosa and this further increased their influence.

Wu-Hsin and Rü-Hui now placed their evidence before these two men and a sum of money collected by Miao-Chi's enemies was promised them. The two elders did not need much persuasion. For a long time they had resented Miao-Chi, this ascetic zealot who, by his self-sacrificing life and powerful religious preaching, was turning Buddhist society upside down. It would give them boundless satisfaction to clear him out. They would have him publicly expelled from Buddhist society and branded as a heretic and a dishonest fraud. If this method did not succeed they would resort to a more dangerous yet efficient means of discrediting him by denouncing him to the authorities as a political traitor.

It was not long before a demand was made for an extraordinary meeting of the Council of Elders to deal with Miao-Chi's case. A message was sent to the authorities of Fa Yün Ssu requesting them to attend in the capital. The Abbot, Deputy Abbot, Man-T'u and Ta-Hsuan were chosen as representatives. In addition there came one or two representatives from each of the larger monasteries on the island. The Abbot and his monks had already heard through Hsü-Shan how things stood. They were all sad and several of them were angry because of Miao-Chi's unguarded words but their deepest feeling was a desire to help their esteemed colleague out of his difficulties. This was the feeling too with the majority of representatives from other places. In their hearts lay an admiration for this unusual monk who dared to stake so much for truth. It was this note that marked the beginning of the council meeting.

Soon another note was introduced. With an important air the lawyer monk set out the evidence which had been compiled. There could be no doubt, he concluded, that Miao-Chi was not only a heretic but a fraud; indeed a shameful blot on Buddhist society in Formosa. Then the Abbot of Fa Yün Ssu took the floor. "We willingly admit," he said, "that Miao-Chi may have been unduly zealous in his plans for reform, and it is only natural that many resent his liberal outlook which borders on Christianity. But we know that tolerance towards other religions and different ways of thought is a characteristic of Mahayana Buddhism. T'ai-Hsü has even said that if Christians did not insist on the idea of a personal God he would not hesitate to regard Christianity as a Western form of Mahayana. Furthermore, everyone in this assembly knows from his own conscience that if there is anyone amongst us who lives according to the demands of religion as a self-denying work for others it is Miao-Chi. This indictment has clearly been prepared by people who wish to cause his downfall. I submit that there is no proof of these accusations and if they are taken before the court it will be a bad day for the accusers." A burst of applause broke out from many parts of the hall but a small group sat rigid and unbending. The

Abbot continued, "If Miao-Chi has gone too far I suggest that the Council of Elders caution him, or decide that for a time he leave Lung Shan Ssu in order to recover himself, either here in Formosa or across in the Province of Fukien." The Deputy Abbot expressed himself in similar terms and he was strongly supported by several prominent monks and lay scholars. The battle seemed already lost for the opposition.

Then the lay Buddhist, T'ang, rose to his feet. He was red with passion and there was an ominous gleam in his eyes. He exploded his bomb: "So this is how you handle the case of an obvious heretic and fraud! There is nothing to be done except to lay before you another document. From reliable sources it has been learned that Miao-Chi is in contact with subversive elements at home and abroad; his Communistic tendencies come out clearly in his writings. Can this be explained away? Let me remind you that we live in a country where such things carry serious consequences."

This was plain speaking; everybody knew what was in question, and it was superfluous to send the new document of accusation round the assembly, but T'ang insisted that everyone should see it. The bomb had done its work. No one dared open his mouth after this.

Miao-Chi heard the result next day. He knew what it meant but remained quiet and composed, for a new peace was beginning to fill his heart. The most important thing was to get his loyal group of students away lest they too should become involved. Miao-Chi had to use all his powers of persuasion to secure it. Next morning they gathered at the railway station and after the train had left it was a lonely man who returned slowly to the deserted temple. He felt that he ought not to leave it even to visit the Mission; that might appear too much like an attempt at escape if the Japanese police came along.

Day after day passed and no one appeared. He had ample time for meditation and prayer and again he worked through the Pauline letters. These brought him encouragement because they had been written by a man familiar with prisons and suffering for the sake of Christ.

In the meantime the Japanese chief-of-police was at work. He called in a number of Japanese monks in order to hear their opinion of Miao-Chi. It appeared that they knew him and most of them held him in high regard. Several of them had collaborated with him in the periodical and they all acknowledged his splendid religious and social work. Instead, therefore, of an ordinary policeman coming to Lung Shan Ssu to fetch Miao-Chi a small group of Japanese monks arrived. It had been arranged that he should not be taken to prison but to a Japanese temple where he would be isolated during a period of investigation. No one would be allowed to see him and no letter could be received or sent.

The lay Buddhist, T'ang, and the disaffected monks who had led the attack had a spy in the neighbourhood of the temple in order to learn what was happening inside. When they learned that Japanese monks had taken Miao-Chi away they received a shock; evidently he was not to be treated as a common criminal. For safety's sake they thought it best to leave as quietly as possible. The following week the whole company of them took passage to Amoy. Thus it happened that the main witnesses failed to appear when the first investigation was held. This did not mean setting Miao-Chi free because the Japanese system of justice was slow and complicated. He remained confined, cut off from the rest of the world.

In the early summer of 1929 I was again able to visit Formosa. For a long time nothing had been heard from Miao-Chi and my letters remained unanswered. None of his friends dared to write and tell me about his fate. When I arrived at the Mission in Taipeh my first inquiry was about Miao-Chi. I then heard that following my last visit he had often been present at services and meetings but for the last few months no one had seen anything of him. They had no notion of his whereabouts. I went to Lung Shan Ssu and there met a new monk in charge who was courteous but non-committal; it was impossible to get anything out of him except that Miao-Chi had gone away, he didn't know where. His nervous manner showed that he did not speak the truth. I tried to obtain information at other temples but everywhere received the same reply. In order to understand this mysterious silence it has to be remembered that the population of Formosa had learnt discretion through bitter experience of Japanese rule. A single item of information about someone under arrest often meant serious complications for those concerned. Naturally I was regarded with suspicion.

I decided to travel to Fa Yün Ssu, the chief monastery, where I felt certain of obtaining reliable information. Early one morning I set off with a Danish colleague and a Chinese Christian friend, first by train to Piao Miao and then aboard a trolley along the switchback towards Ta Hu. We travelled through a fearful thunderstorm, and were soon drenched to the skin as we raced along the valleys and over swaying bridges above the torrents. All the way a Japanese and a Formosan followed us at a distance. We guessed who they were.

About three in the afternoon the sun broke through, we were able to dry our clothes, and a wonderful opportunity was afforded us of seeing the Great Lake itself, the village and neighbouring valleys in a constantly-moving colour play. To the east rose the mountain ranges of Formosa, their majestic ridges and peaks rising fifteen thousand feet above sea level. Up there live the tribes, robust and agile people, who still occasionally indulge in the sport of head hunting. Some of the more peaceful among them sometimes come down to Ta Hu village to sell produce.

One or two of the younger monks soon spotted us and reported our arrival. The Abbot was absent in the island capital, but Man-T'u, the instructor, and Ta-Hsuan, the host, were there. It was possibly with mixed feelings that they saw their former acquaintance from the Brotherhood in Nanking come up the broad steps, but their embarrassment was soon over and they gave us a hearty reception. Soon we were being served with a delicious vegetarian meal, and how good it tasted after our exacting journey!

Afterwards we were led into the main hall. This was illuminated in a festive way with candles and lamps and all the monks were present. Ta-Hsuan first offered a hearty greeting of welcome and then Man-T'u took the floor and spoke with glowing enthusiasm of the Brotherhood at Nanking and what it had meant for him. Not a word was said about Miao-Chi, for seated in a corner were the two detectives listening. Still, there was probably no one who did not feel that it was Miao-Chi who in a mysterious way bound us together. Afterwards Ta-Hsuan asked me to speak and emphasized that I had the whole evening at my disposal. It was a valuable opportunity for me to explain the inner meaning of life in the light of Christ Jesus. Man-T'u stood by my side and translated into Fukien dialect. It was convenient to have a blackboard handy because numerous questions were asked and there were many points that needed written as well as oral explanation. After an hour and a half I suggested a pause but they preferred to continue. The gathering went on until a late hour with readings from the New Testament and our liturgy. They were particularly enthusiastic about our worship and I was called upon to chant various liturgical passages for them.

When the monks finally dispersed and the detectives had disappeared we were led to the guest-room by our two hosts. A large mosquito-net had been suspended from the beams and we were to lie on mats with multi-coloured Japanese blankets over us. The two monks had another reason for accompanying us. They knew that my mind was filled with anxiety concerning the fate of Miao-Chi. Anxiously they looked around and when they were sure that no strangers were present they began to speak in whispers. There followed a graphic and colourful account of Miao-Chi's development after I had left him. They described his courageous and frank demeanour, the opposition, intrigue and the final arrest. After this, they said, it was impossible to make contact with Miao-Chi and no one dared to speak about him lest there be more trouble. They begged me not to mention anything about Miao-Chi, not even to missionary friends. This I promised and in return they promised to convey to him my personal greetings as soon as his case had been settled and normal relationships resumed.

I lay awake a good while praying for my friend, but when dawn broke a sure conviction entered my mind that Miao-Chi would come through victorious for Christ.

The investigations in connection with his case were protracted; it was not until the autumn of 1929 that a verdict was given. He was acquitted on all points and it was expressly added that he should be reinstated in his former position. Detailed information on how Miao-Chi fared during the six long months of the investigation was lacking but we learned that he had been treated with consideration by the Japanese monks. The long confinement and the anxiety had certainly left their marks upon him. On the other hand, quiet hours of meditation had enabled him to think over life's problems and make plans for the future.

The Council of Elders met immediately after the verdict and drew up a statement expressing profound satisfaction at the decision and requesting Miao-Chi to resume his former post. He, however, thought otherwise. During his isolation he had come to view many things in a different light, and he saw clearly that it would be impossible for someone who had become a Christian to accept such a position. The same consideration was decisive regarding the editorship of *Asia's Light*. After much struggle Miao-Chi had reached the conclusion that even this, his dearest child, must be sacrificed and so the periodical ceased publication. He felt that he needed time for renewal, and in the home of his brother a room was always ready. A short course at the Normal College in Taipeh would make it possible for him to become a teacher. Above all he longed for recreation on the mountains and expressed a wish to stay for a while at Fa Yün Ssu without undertaking any duties.

25

Under Stress of Illness

THE FIRST WEEKS Miao-Chi spent in his brother's home appear to have been happy. Lo Chi-Ying had made remarkable progress in religious understanding and power. He had found too that Christianity is the religion that meets all the needs of man for this life and eternity. Miao-Chi's stay with his brother and his excellent wife and their happy children brought edification and strengthening.

They discussed arrangements for the future and were agreed that a teacher's work was the best occupation for Miao-Chi; it would give him opportunity to reach many with the message now burning in his soul. They decided that he should start at the Normal College immediately after New Year when a shorter course would begin for advanced students. There was, however, a shadow over their reunion; Miao-Chi was no longer the robust man that he was previously. He had become short of breath and over his drawn face lay marks of suffering. As soon as possible he sought out Dr. McClure of the Mission Hospital who told him to rest, preferably in a high altitude, and eat nourishing food. He also gave him some tonic medicine.

Miao-Chi therefore accepted an invitation to go up to Fa Yün Ssu. Besides he hoped to get opportunities of doing more for his monkish friends and to share with them his vision of Christ as the Light of the World. He was welcomed at the monastery and in a short time was busily occupied with lectures.

My informant was a monk who visited us towards the end of 1929 and who intended having two years of study in China. He had followed Miao-Chi's lectures for several weeks and felt deeply stirred by his glowing power and zeal. Miao-Chi had expressly asked him to visit our Brotherhood to bring his warm

K

greetings and to let me know how things stood. He had added, "Stay for some days in the Brotherhood and take part with them in their worship. Remember there is no one like Christ."

At the outset the period spent on the mountain was good. Monks of all ages gathered around Miao-Chi and many became spiritually awakened and renewed. For the young especially Miao-Chi appeared as a martyr. What made the most profound impression perhaps was that no word of bitterness or revenge passed his lips. On the contrary he said frequently "Let us remember those words of the Apostle Paul, 'All things work together for good to them that love God.'"[1]

New Year 1930 was approaching, and Miao-Chi had begun preparations for returning to Taipeh and his new studies. An unusually sharp spell of cold weather set in during New Year and Miao-Chi contracted a heavy cold. He ran a high temperature and had to go to bed. Several weeks passed but his cold refused to get better. When a little blood came up in his sputum it suggested to him and others that it might be tuberculosis of the lungs, that dread disease which carries off so many Buddhist monks and students in Asia.

As soon as Miao-Chi recovered sufficiently to go out he travelled to Taipeh, but it was then well into February and too late to think of a course of teacher training. Besides, his strength was so weak it would have been impossible for him to carry on serious studies. It was evident that a stay in hospital was needed. He went first to the Red Cross Hospital as he knew that they were reluctant to receive t.b. patients at the Mission Hospital, but the medical supervision and treatment were poor; further, there were few or no Christians with whom he could converse, and this had become one of the most important things for him. He turned again to Dr. McClure asking that an exception be made in the Hospital's rules. This was granted, and so it came about that Miao-Chi began to spend some weeks in wholly Christian surroundings.

Now he was in his proper element, occupied with his precious Bible, in talks with missionaries and the hospital evangelist and taking part regularly in the morning and evening services. The evangelist and leaders became very fond of this thoughtful and devoted man and often asked him to take part in their meetings. This he did very gladly, and all found it enriching and uplifting.

[1] Rom. 8: 28.

With increasing happiness and peace he went on preaching until he had to take to his bed.

Another important work absorbed his time and that was writing letters to friends and disciples both in Formosa and China. These letters had one constant aim, to glorify Jesus the Saviour who gives hope, strength and victory in life and death. "Unfortunately, I did not reach the point," he wrote, "that I could lead every one of you to Him, but now from my sick bed (which may possibly become my death bed) I beg you to seek Him, the great Saviour, through prayer and faith so that you may find happiness for time and eternity."

26

Entry Into Life

IT WAS ABOUT this time that the full realization of death dawned upon Miao-Chi. He had often thought about it. Theoretically this unavoidable process had always been in mind and he believed that he had been able to fit death harmoniously into a pattern of life and eternity.

Sayings on life and death that constantly recurred in Buddhist scriptures had become part of his thinking. "Life and death follow one another as the waves of the ocean. Now we are up on the crest of the wave, now down in the trough, until at last, through a realization of the truth, this process ends and we enter into the great silence." In this mode of thinking, which he had earlier accepted as axiomatic, there was no real sting either in death or life. It was different now that the Christian faith had gripped him. Nor was he quite so sure now of the truth of reincarnation. What if it were only once that we live on this earth, never to return! What if death puts the final full stop to life!

At any rate it was serious to leave earthly life and enter into the unknown. Nor did Miao-Chi have any doubt about what made it so serious. It was sin. It was not for nothing that the Apostle Paul had used those weighty words, "The sting of death is sin."[1]

The thought of death had not played any important part in his earlier religious life. What had predominated was a wish for clarity and understanding of life and how to get into right relations with all living beings. He still felt that this was an important aspect of life but there was one aspect even more important, to get right with God, to become at one with Him and obtain full faith in the forgiveness of sin.

He remembered his cosmic awakening in Japan, when he had

[1] I Cor. 15: 56.

had a certain feeling of shame because he had led a life so ego-centric, but any deeper sorrow and pain he had not noticed and there had been no thought of any forgiveness of sin. It was different now that he had come closer to Christ. He began to look into an abyss of uncleanness and sin. His life lay before him like an open book and on every page stood recorded, "You have always sought your own good and your own glory. You have not feared, loved and honoured your God and Creator as you ought to have done. You have been a guide to others without knowing the way yourself. It is all failure, all patchwork. You have not helped others in what they most needed, to get right about sin and per-sonal surrender to God."

He thought of his life in the temple, of many conscience-laden people who had come to offer sacrifice, of many bewildered folk who wanted assurance regarding the unknown future. How sorely they needed to hear of the atonement which had been effected through Christ on Calvary! Yet the only thing he had been able to give them was a confused indication of a problematic and mythical All-Father Buddha who had given his vows of mercy about the Pure Land. An unspeakable sorrow filled his soul, and now he might soon die, unclean and burdened in conscience, and pass over the river into the great unknown. Hour after hour he lay there in fear and anguish. Where lay the solution?

Suddenly a memory flashed into his mind. What was it that his Western friend had said in the temple more than two years ago? It was one of the last things emphasized during their closing devotions: "The Spirit of God who has begun this work in your soul will surely lead you safely through the decisive crisis that must come. Don't be afraid of having that settlement of your conscience with God, even if it proves stern and difficult, because it will lead to the real break-through to abundant life in God. Remember in such an hour how important it is to speak frankly with Christian friends."

Miao-Chi remembered certain verses which his friend had told him to underline in his Bible, e.g. concerning binding and loosing,[1] and the power of Christian prayer.[2] He made the decision there and then; he called the hospital evangelist and asked him to send urgently for two missionary friends. He had suddenly

---

[1] Matt. 18: 18.   [2] James 5: 14–16.

become aware that sickness unto death was almost certainly God's challenge of grace. The two friends came and stayed with him the whole night. It was one spent in earnest conversation and prayer, a night of struggle and reckoning in God's sight, a night when the powerful words of the Apostle Paul on being "set right through faith" again showed their relevance and efficacy. Before dawn Miao-Chi had found liberty and peace in Christ. He had been released from sorrow and fear and had experienced the utter joy of forgiveness of sin.

The next day his first act was to send out a public declaration that he had become a Christian. Afterwards followed a number of letters to friends and acquaintances whom he wished to share in his happiness. Orthodox Buddhists were surprised and indignant, and in a Buddhist newspaper in Taipeh some days later appeared a paragraph saying that Lo Miao-Chi might now be reckoned dead in that he had renounced Buddhism and become a Christian. Paul the Apostle would have rejoined, Yes, dead to his old self and risen to new life in Christ Jesus![1]

The weeks became filled with joyful triumph and this seemed to bring new fire and vigour to his emaciated body. It almost looked as if he might take a turn for the better. His testimonies at meetings became even more gripping and many who visited him left with a profound impression of divine power as it shone from his face. For the brothers, Chi-Ying and Fu-Ying, who often visited him, these interviews became of revolutionary importance, for they too had now decided to become Christians together with their households. To his father he wrote a letter describing vividly his experience and concluding with the wish that his father too might reach a similar joy. Many Buddhist friends visited him and for each and every one he had a thrilling and helpful word. This I heard of repeatedly during the following years when Buddhist monks visited our Brotherhood from Formosa, and there was not one among them who had not heard of Lo Miao-Chi's wonderful testimony to richness of life in Christ.

Again he caught a chill, and again his temperature rose quickly. As Miao-Chi's strength declined it became clear that his end was not far off. There was no hope that he could be baptized in church, and, according to what I have been able to ascertain, his baptism must have taken place in the sickroom.

[1] Rom. 6: 5–11.

Miao-Chi died quietly on April 20, 1930. He was, of course, accorded Christian burial and there was a mighty gathering of Christians and Buddhists. After one of the missionaries, a Formosan minister and the evangelist of the hospital had expressed what Miao-Chi meant to the Island, his elder brother, Chi-Ying, expressed sincere thanks to the Christian Church where his beloved brother had found a final spiritual home. He spoke of what Miao-Chi had been to the home of their childhood, and of his remarkable development through the years until finally he had reached salvation, power and light in Christ Jesus. The remarks resolved themselves into a testimony, for he ended by saying, "Miao-Chi always showed us the way. We always felt secure in following him, for he was always 'of the truth', so we shall continue to follow him."

The Buddhists too arranged a memorial service and several Christians attended. It almost seemed as if Christians and Buddhists had found one another over the grave of our friend. Dr. R. B. McClure in a letter to me remarks, "As a professed Christian Miao-Chi lived for only a short time, but he was a man who in truth and spirit followed the Master when he at last decided to take this step", and we may add that, although his full time of Christian service was so brief, he became of unique and lasting importance for the coming of the Kingdom, not least among the Buddhists of Formosa. They still speak of him and his victorious entry into life.

What makes Miao-Chi's life story so instructive is primarily the fact that we can follow his development. His early experiences were important, as were his "cosmic-awakening" and the awareness of a calling that made him spend himself willingly in order to deliver men from superstition and weakness. Nevertheless it all pales before his last experience when, through an honest reckoning with life, he gave himself wholly to God in faith. Miao-Chi thereby reached a level where the greatest men of religion have found renewal; on the one side God's boundless power, holiness and majesty, causing man to shrink in guilt, and on the other an awareness of God's love and grace for the sinner who truly seeks His presence. This experience liberates man, transforms his entire existence and gives him a vision of devoted service for the salvation of the world.

BIOGRAPHICAL NOTE

T'ai-Hsü

THE MAN WHO unquestionably exercised greatest influence on Buddhism during the last generation was T'ai-Hsü, Miao-Chi's famous teacher. His figure became known and respected all over Asia, while in Europe and America there are students of comparative religion who know of him—some of whom had the opportunity of hearing his lectures when he visited Berlin, London, Paris and New York in 1928.

T'ai-Hsü was born in 1888 in the Province of Chekiang, not far from the city of Hangchow, near the Hsi Hu ("West Lake"). Hangchow and its surroundings possess the richest collection imaginable of monasteries, pagodas and beautiful pavilions. Religious solemnity and aesthetic dignity pervade the entire neighbourhood. T'ai-Hsü, with rich endowments of mind and receptive senses, absorbed something of this Hangchow atmosphere.

The young T'ai-Hsü soon came into contact with the radical political ideas that were becoming prevalent at the turn of the century in China. At fifteen he had become an agitator among political reformers but soon found it necessary to disappear from the political arena, and this was certainly one of the reasons why he chose monastic life. Further, in the life around Hangchow he had absorbed a good deal of Buddhist influence and felt spiritually related to several *fa-shih* who were noted for scholarship. The main reason why he chose monastic life was possibly the growing feeling of pessimism and disillusionment that so easily comes over youth when it encounters life's disappointments.

He made such progress in his monastic studies that at the age of twenty he founded the first centre for scientific study of Buddhism. He went to Nanking for a time and collaborated with the famous scholar Yang Wen-Hui,[1] and then began travelling in order to deliver lectures at the main Buddhist centres. He stayed for a while in Peking with the famous abbot Tao-Kai, who, although a close friend of the Imperial House, possessed considerable understanding of the reforms that T'ai-Hsü had in mind.

It was after his visit to Peking that T'ai-Hsü founded a Buddhist study group that later developed into a nation-wide Buddhist Society, and he became its first president. By this time he had realized his abilities as a stylist and organizer. On the one hand he saw clearly the store of unutilized values in Buddhist scriptures and culture; on the other he sensed the decline of Buddhist society. Large numbers of monks had sunk into ignorance and worldliness, many of the monasteries were ruined by hordes of soldier-bandits, and worship in the temples had become marked by superstition and magic so that educated people felt repelled. Over against these T'ai-Hsü was aware of freer religious associations, not least Protestant and Roman Catholic Missions, which were making great strides with their schools, colleges, hospitals and orphanages. Buddhism was being put in the shade. He felt that for a reformation to be successful external power was necessary; neither learning nor literary style nor piety was sufficient. It was also clear that the work of reformation would meet stubborn opposition, not only from wide circles of monks but chiefly from influential leaders—the abbots, the *fa-shih* and powerful guardians of monastic property.

The opportunity came with the year of revolution in 1911 when T'ai-Hsü had completed his twenty-third year. His plan was for revolutionaries to occupy one of the chief Buddhist centres and from there begin cleaning up. Choice fell upon Golden Mount Monastery, near Chinkiang.[2] As central and dominating as a mediaeval castle, it was an ideal place for a daring coup. T'ai-Hsü and his friends undertook the adventure full of youthful enthusiasm. He was given a detachment of troops and soon the monastery was occupied. Its halls were turned into offices and classrooms for the education of reformist leaders. T'ai-Hsü issued despatches and proclamations and made journeys to Nanking where China's first president, Dr. Sun Yat-Sen, exercised his office for a few short months.

Difficulties soon arose within the revolutionary movement.

[1] See Chapter 11.   [2] See Chapter 9.

The students wanted to have their say, and the majority of them had no interest whatsoever in preserving China's religions. On the contrary, they maintained that religions, and above all Buddhism, were breeding-grounds for conservatism and reaction. In certain places temples and monasteries were plundered and Buddhist images publicly burnt or thrown into the rivers. Several tragedies took place both in town and country where stubborn monks tried to barricade themselves against temple raiders. When the reactionaries, under Yuan Shih-Kai's leadership, came into power T'ai-Hsü realized that the game was up as one after another of his revolutionary friends disappeared. Disguised and depressed he fled to Shanghai and then, by the help of Buddhists, took passage for P'u T'o Island. Here he found refuge in a small monastery where he was allowed to *pi-kuan*, i.e. live in a locked cell for a number of years. In 1913 he thus became dead to the world.

The idea of *pi-kuan* is that a monk may be given opportunity to rehabilitate himself by concentrated meditation and thorough study of the Buddhist scriptures. Long meditations were not according to T'ai-Hsü's mind but studies were simply life to him and he looked forward to having time for writing too. From the monastic library he had brought Buddhist writings. Paper and Chinese ink he regularly obtained through the little trap-door that opened and shut whenever food was pushed in for him. In the cell were a bed, a bench to sit on, a table with writing instruments and chopsticks, an extra table for books and a small altar in one corner with an image of Buddha. In the yard, just large enough to allow him a little exercise, were a small flower-bed and a few water jars. The water supply came through a long bamboo pipe from the mountain stream beyond. A couple of poles were set up with a string for laundry and in one corner of the yard the necessary "little room" had been erected.

The silence was accentuated by the rush of the tide as it flowed in and out among the sandbanks of P'u T'o Island. This made a profound impression upon T'ai-Hsü as may be seen in the name of the Buddhist periodical *Hai Chao Yin* (*Rising Tide*) which he founded. He spent the first three years mainly in study and writing. Notes, summaries and essays piled up. During the last year he spent hours in thought, because it was important to reach clarity regarding future plans of work.

Those four years influenced T'ai-Hsü profoundly. In spite of the fact that he looked like a savage, with long unkempt hair and beard, a new peace of mind had settled upon him. He saw that his revolutionary dreams had not led to the expected goal. On the contrary, through his immaturity and ignorance, he had led both himself and others into unfortunate entanglements. The rationalistic Wei Shih philosophy prevented him from being troubled by self-reproaches and pangs of conscience; he would continue to labour for reform, but it would be done without fanaticism and with careful consideration for the circumstances of life. Moderation, self-control, wisdom and a clear outlook should, from now onwards, become his watchwords. By contrast with so many *pi-kuan* monks T'ai-Hsü came out of his isolation without having experienced any "cosmic-awakening". It is significant that his later activity was marked by a decided rationalism. On the other hand, there is no doubt that he grew considerably in strength of characer and balance of outlook.

At first most people imagined that T'ai-Hsü had shared the fate of other unfortunate leaders of the revolution who had been secretly removed from this world. Quite a number of the more conservative members of Buddhist society would have been glad if this had been true; indeed the wave of indignation against him had run so high that his place of refuge was kept secret. After three years it began to leak out that T'ai-Hsü had entered a cell for an indefinite period, that he regretted his rashness and was now busily engaged in cleansing his heart through studies and spiritual exercises. If there is anything that impresses Chinese Buddhists it is a permanent or temporary forsaking of this world. It means that one's conversion is serious. Indignation soon began to subside and his friends accordingly availed themselves of the press in order to rehabilitate his reputation. There appeared notices in the papers about T'ai-Hsü's forthcoming contribution towards Buddhism. He had been interviewed through the trap-door of his cell and questioners had been struck by his sincerity.

On the day of his rehabilitation all the abbots and dignitaries on P'u T'o Shan, together with other prominent Buddhist scholars, appeared and walked in procession to the monastery. Salvoes of firecrackers were discharged and a solemn mass was offered in front of his cell. Then the red seal was removed by the abbot and the hero was led out and acclaimed with enthusiasm. A busy time now began for T'ai-Hsü. A beginning was made in Shanghai, the place where influential Buddhist laymen often gather. Lectures were given, conferences held and the new periodical *Rising Tide* shot up like a brilliant rocket into the literary sky. His manuscripts were printed and sold among the bookshops of Shanghai. Invitations came from Japan, and by the end of 1917 T'ai-Hsü had become a guest of honour in some of the famous monasteries of Tokyo and Kyoto. He began to see clearly that he had a great task before him, not only in China but in the whole of Asia and in other parts of the world. Back in China he eagerly continued his travels and literary work. Faithful to his resolution, T'ai-Hsü made contacts everywhere with prominent Buddhist laymen. They on their part supplied him with necessary means, introduced him to higher officials and supported his plans. At the same time several of the younger and better-educated monks of reformist tendencies began to join him. They constituted themselves his bodyguard and rejoiced in his light, well knowing that they would in this way have chances of promotion in the new China. With his keen understanding of men it was easy for T'ai-Hsü to place these enthusiastic monks in key positions in editorial offices and in temples and monasteries of liberal outlook. This was probably one of the chief reasons for his success during those years. He picked out intelligent young monks to follow him on lecture tours as a team of secretaries and reporters. Some of these journeys became triumphal processions, especially along the coast and up the Yangtse valley. In the Wuhan cities an extraordinary revival took place, and thousands of men and women, some from the highest levels of society, became T'ai-Hsü's disciples. No wonder that Wuchang became the centre for his first and most important academy.[1]

The author first came into contact with T'ai-Hsü at Kuling in 1924. He received me with kindness and when he understood that I had pursued some studies in comparative religion he became very interested. He willingly conceded that through Christianity a new and quickening impulse had entered the spiritual life of the East. "It is felt everywhere", he said, "religiously, socially and morally. It is impossible to get away from the remarkable power that has radiated from Christ, that remarkable *bodhisattva*." When we were discussing the Fourth Gospel he once remarked, "It is surely correct to say that *Tao* (Divine Wisdom) was incarnate in

[1] See Chapters 14–16.

Jesus Christ in a special way, but now the main thing is that *Tao* should be incarnate in us too!" Matters developed so that T'ai-Hsü and I could meet as friends; not that we became more agreed in our views—on the contrary our divergence in religious outlook became more pronounced. There are probably few with whom I have discussed religion more than with T'ai-Hsü but, although he was always an honest sceptic and a fair opponent, he did not hesitate to tell me that he considered Christianity to be inferior to Buddhism. He found the doctrine of the one personal God as the origin of all life quite unacceptable. Neither could he reconcile himself to prayer, for to him everything follows fixed laws and we form our own destiny. Thus he remained a stranger to the power and blessing of faith and prayer.

Whenever I think of the gifted T'ai-Hsü a profound saying of our Lord Jesus comes to mind: "If therefore the light that is in thee be darkness, how great is that darkness" (Matt. 6: 23). By the end of the War he was a broken man. During a Japanese air attack on the suburbs of Chungking he suffered bomb shock from which he never wholly recovered. He died in 1947.